508.777 I64
Iowa : portrait of the land
50204

WITHDRAWN

EARTH DAY
April 22, 2000

Fellow Iowans,

This book is a gift for the people of Iowa. It is a portrait of our state's land and its resources, as we see them today and as they were originally. This remarkable view of our home state through time is meant to challenge you to think about what could be here in the future.

We all touch the earth, whether we're farmers who work the soil or other citizens whose spirits are enriched simply by living in Iowa's fertile land. That common thread, spun of a common heritage, has been woven into the tightly knit fabric of community. We pride ourselves on being Iowans, and we share more similarities than differences. Our identity and our citizenship come, in part, from running our fingers and our lives through that bountiful, beautiful land between two rivers.

Yet people are just part of this bounty – a few of the many strands in a web of plants, animals, earth, water, and air that make up the larger, diverse environment of Iowa. Enhancing the quality of life in Iowa depends upon our ability to maintain and improve those ageless connections. Iowans will become better stewards of the land by understanding its geological foundations, preserving its rich soil, recognizing its native habitats and species, safeguarding its waters, protecting its air resources, and conserving its ancient and historic cultural sites.

We hope *Iowa – Portrait of the Land* will connect Iowans with the land's history and with their responsibility to pass on this heritage in good condition to future generations. We also hope this book will first step in planning how we will use and protect our resources in the future. As we begin that process, we welcome your ideas, comments, and suggestions.

Sincerely,

Thomas J. Vilsack
GOVERNOR OF IOWA

Sally J. Pederson
LT. GOVERNOR

D1508382

620205

508,777
I64

5,00

IOWA - Portrait of the Land

EARTH DAY
APRIL 22, 2000

Iowa Department of Natural Resources
STATE OF IOWA

050204

State of Iowa, Des Moines 50319
Copyright © 2000 by the
Iowa Department of Natural Resources
All rights reserved
Printed in Iowa
First edition, 2000

No part of this book may be reproduced
or utilized in any form or by any means,
electronic or mechanical, including photocopying
and recording, without permission in writing
from the publisher.

Printed on acid-free, recycled paper

Library of Congress Control Number: 00-026091

International Standard Book Number
0-9678786-0-8 (pbk.)

CONTENTS

FOREWORD

My family and I have just filled our woodshed with white oak. The good oak came from a 208-year-old witness tree on the ridge above our Upper Iowa River valley farm. What an amazing transformation of land and culture that tree lived through before it died a couple years ago.

Our oak began life at a time when passenger pigeons were so abundant that they darkened the sky during their autumn migrations. We're told that the pigeons would engorge themselves with acorns and then regurgitate them as they roosted at night. Was our oak the result of one of those migratory dispersals?

Our oak was forty-two years old when Nathan Boone, son of Daniel, surveyed the Upper Iowa River and laid out a territory called the Neutral Ground that became a temporary home for the Winnebago (Ho-Chunk) Indians. It wasn't long, however, before a Yankee born in New York in 1790, the same year as our oak, laid claim to the land – and our farm was born.

During the next fifty years our oak witnessed perhaps the most rapid transformation of any landscape in the history of the world. Iowa in the 1840s consisted of 28 million acres of tallgrass prairie interspersed with large and small wetlands and 7 million acres of forest. By 1900 almost all of the prairie was replaced by 200,000 farms. The wetlands were sucked dry by hundreds of thousands of miles of drain tile, and more than two-thirds of the forests were converted to firewood, railroad ties, fence posts, houses, and barns.

By the time our oak reached middle age, Iowa's last mountain lion, bison, black bear, elk, wolf, whooping crane, sandhill crane, and trumpeter swan had disappeared. In 1914 the last of the passenger pigeons, surrogate parents of oaks, died in a Cincinnati zoo.

As the twentieth century began, our oak looked down over the valley to see Iowa's first hydroelectric plant light up the night sky. That event also marked the last time northern pike swam freely from the Mississippi up past our farm. Iowa was growing richer in power, people, railroads, and farms but inversely poorer in things natural, wild, and free.

The winds of the next quarter-century must have made our oak shudder with sadness. Farm fields grew smaller as gullies divided them into ever-smaller pieces. Even deer, turkey, and beaver disappeared. Soil instead of passenger pigeons darkened Iowa's sky and replaced the pike and other species in our rivers and streams.

During the last seventy years of our oak's life, Iowa began to grow up and settle down, and Iowans' understanding of their place in the land community began to mature. Forests, parks, and wildlife refuges were established. The soil conservation movement began. The river became cleaner as Iowans took more responsibility for their personal and community behavior. Deer, turkey, beaver, otters, eagles, sandhill cranes, and trumpeter swans returned.

Our oak lived through an amazing era in Iowa's history. It put down deeper roots, lifted its arms higher, and endured more Iowa weather than any of us or our families can claim. Although it no longer stands tall above our river valley, its progeny and the land community it belonged to live on. We merge with its story as we live out our lives.

Iowa – Portrait of the Land is also a story about this land we call Iowa and our place in it. It has been written to encourage you to think about what our oak witnessed and about how we've come to be what we are today. But even more importantly, it has been written to start you thinking about what kind of land our oak's offspring will witness. That will be up to you.

It is now your turn to help paint our portrait on the land. You will add color every day as you make personal and community decisions on how you live. We at the Iowa Department of Natural Resources, along with the many other conservation-minded organizations and individuals across our state, hope you will help paint a landscape in which our children and all of creation can thrive.

Paul W. Johnson
DIRECTOR
Iowa Department of Natural Resources

A LOOK AT THE LAND
Essay and photo by Drake Hokanson

Perhaps more than any other state, Iowa is land; great, rolling reaches of it, blunt as a workboot, fine-textured as Japanese paper. Georgia has its piedmont, Arizona its rock desert, but Iowa has – Iowa is – *land*. Everything that grows on it gratefully pushes roots into its dark soil; everything that humans build on it casts small shadows across its great presence. Land is to Iowa as water is to the sea, the one essential thing.

I crossed Iowa by small plane recently, from the southwest corner to northeast corner; Lincoln, Nebraska, to La Crosse, Wisconsin. I flew low, about 3,000 feet above the soil, because I wanted to see this wide state pass close beneath. On a warm day from so low you can sometimes *smell* the earth. But on this June day it had rained; the fields were quiet, and I suspected the cafes full of farmers on short furlough. Woodbine to Auburn, Badger to Clear Lake, Orchard to Lime Springs, I had the privilege of a rare diagonal, an angled route across the grain of Iowa's window-screen grid of section-line roads.

First were the arrow-point Loess Hills that rose from the broad Missouri floodplain; the hills expanded outward to become the sides of a close valley: the Boyer River valley, thinly wooded as if trees had only recently found it. Then the river faded into the up-lands, the broad turtle-back of the Des Moines Lobe, where melting ice left broad lands that cried out for twelve-row corn planters.

After a stop in Clear Lake for fuel, I watched those long, straight rivers – the Shell Rock, the Cedar, the Wapsipinicon – bear off to the southeast, like arrows in a quiver, pointing toward the great river out of sight past the Earth's curve. Mile by mile I watched corn and roads, corn and farmsteads, corn and soybeans, towns and land pass beneath. I looked for the ragged little square of Hayden Prairie near Lime Springs, but missed it in the expanse.

There is nothing bold about Iowa's land – except its extent. Its charms are quiet ones, requiring much of the observer. You must look with an eye for the gentle horizon line, the subtle shadings of soil, the exclamation points of trees and distant grain elevators. Iowa is the land, and it is enough.

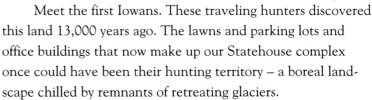

Olive hairstreak butterfly

Pasque flower

The Fabric of Iowa's Land

son

LOOK AGAIN . . .

As you admire Iowa's fertile fields, tidy homes, busy cities, and network of roads, consider the links that connect our land, our people, and our history. Sometimes eloquently, sometimes more subtly, today's images also speak of our past.

At our State Capitol, Iowans may stand in awe of the golden dome, chat with their citizen legislators, or feel the energy of people at work in the seat of state government. But when you climb "the hill," try to sense another era as well. Shiver at the frigid breezes off the glacier that piled the dirt and stones beneath your feet. Listen for the roar of meltwater churning down the Des Moines and Raccoon River valleys off to the south. Visualize cool forests of spruce and fir, with open meadows fringing boggy pools left by ice that finally is melting after centuries of glacial cold.

Imagine a dozen human figures, clad in animal skins, stalking through the trees, silently approaching a huge mastodon browsing at the edge of a clearing. The great animal with long tusks, muscular trunk, and shaggy hide means food, as well as danger, to these nomads. If they can kill the beast with their flint-tipped lances, they and their band will eat well for many weeks.

Meet the first Iowans. These traveling hunters discovered this land 13,000 years ago. The lawns and parking lots and office buildings that now make up our Statehouse complex once could have been their hunting territory – a boreal landscape chilled by remnants of retreating glaciers.

The ancient people must have shivered through bitter winters that would have made modern Iowa Januaries seem balmy in comparison. The brief summers brought some warmth, along with the perils of floodwaters. Runoff from the melting glaciers turned the rivers into muddy, pounding torrents filled with tumbling boulders and swirling gravel. Ponder that on a June day when you glide along a placid Iowa stream in your canoe.

Or picture if you can, another place, another era. A herd of shaggy bison is grazing on a hill above a paved highway filled with a rush of traffic. Plodding and chewing, dust swirling around their hooves, the animals stretch out across the grasslands, even beyond the rows of livestock confinement buildings in the distance. If the bison ghosts fade away, count the concrete grain elevators dotting the horizon – and contemplate

Above: Fire was common in the maintenance of the prairie ecosystem prior to Euro-American settlement. (Hoffman Prairie State Preserve, Cerro Gordo County) Left: Earth, water, air, plants, and animals are the basis of Iowa's land resource. (Hendrickson Marsh, Story County)

their unlikely link to a native prairie or forest preserve. Remember that each site stores treasures grown from our rich earth.

Focus your thoughts on an image of neat rows of corn and soybeans planted in the flat, geometric fields of north-central Iowa. But go to those farmlands after a spring rain, when countless shallow ponds and wet swales linger on the black soil. Then envision those potholes bristling with rushes and pond weeds, dappled by the shade of uncounted flocks of ducks and geese and shorebirds circling overhead. No wonder early settlers named nearby towns Mallard, Plover, and Curlew.

2

To experience those wetlands, seek out a friendly farmer's undrained marsh or a state-owned wildlife area. Put on waders or old shoes, then slog through the cattails into the soft mud of the shallows, listening for the buzz of yellow-headed blackbirds and the honks of protesting geese. Use all your senses. Feel the glare of the sun, taste your own perspiration, smell the bubbles of gas stirred up from the decaying vegetation.

Prefer the comfort of an automobile? Watch from your window for stalks of compass plant or clumps of big bluestem waving alongside the road. Think of making that journey across a 28-million-acre expanse of Iowa prairie, bumping along with all your worldly possessions in a canvas-topped wagon.

Do you take Interstate 80 for granted? Be thankful for the modern, raised roadbed across the broad Skunk River flood-plain east of Des Moines. How would you like to have crossed those Skunk River bottoms 150 years ago, when muck and prairie cord grass and mosquitoes seemed to swallow up the covered wagons? Listen, above the drone of diesel engines and humming tires, for the shouts of phantom teamsters urging their oxen through the mud. East Coast magazines warned westbound travelers about that dreaded quagmire they would face in Iowa. Some parties took days to traverse the valley that we now cross in minutes.

In autumn, thousands of people make the pilgrimage to northeast Iowa to savor the spectacle of the changing leaf colors. At Effigy Mounds National Monument, some tourists watch barges and bass anglers on the Mississippi River, while

Jim Heemstra, U.S. Fish and Wildlife Service

Bison lived throughout the native grasslands that included today's Iowa. They were valuable to the American Indians who shared the land. (Neal Smith National Wildlife Refuge, Jasper County)

they listen to the calliope music from an excursion boat. But other visitors may feel the centuries-old spirit of Indian families sculpting a bear effigy from the soil of a blufftop, honoring the earth that sustains all life.

The simplest scene, like dust billowing behind a car on a gravel road, could remind us of our heritage. The rock on that road was crushed from limestone formed by sediment deposited in the shallow seas that covered Iowa 300 to 500 million years

3

*When one tugs at a single thing
in nature he finds it attached
to the rest of the world.
– John Muir*

Tracks preserved in dried mud mark a raccoon's foray in Winneshiek County.

ago. A morning walk along a road can bring many rewards: exercise, a few cents' worth of aluminum beverage cans, and fossils that record ancient geological history.

Even modern farmsteads have roots in our past. Did you ever notice how a new house and steel machine shed perch on a knoll – most likely on the same site where the farm's first owners built their cabin? The slight rise above the surrounding prairie caught the cooling summer breeze and dried out fastest after the wet spring. Or in the hill country of eastern Iowa, see the reflection of the settlers in the homesites they chose. A house on the ridge commanded a view of the neighbors or approaching travelers. The cabin tucked in a sheltered valley brought seclusion and protection from the winter winds. The farmer along the riverbank feared drought more than floods.

Now, of course, the census takers label nearly two-thirds of us "urban" because we live in cities of 2,500 or more. And fewer than 9 percent of Iowans are considered farmers. Yet we can't overlook our rural heritage, our *land* heritage. Many of us have farmers in the family tree or close friends in agribusiness, or we simply may enjoy a ride in the country.

Transplanted to cities and towns, we can't break the habits of our rural ancestry. As you mow your lawn to match the neat carpets maintained by your neighbors, recall the

A morel mushroom pushes to the surface in response to the warmth and humidity of spring. (Sny Magill Valley, Clayton County)

Those pioneers – the Millers, the Olsons, the Van Gundys, the McKinleys – broke the prairie sod and turned it into working land. They and the tireless farmers who followed took advantage of the rich, deep soils and favorable climate to grow grain, cattle, and hogs to feed their families and the world. Their sweat and spirit transformed the wild, bountiful prairies of Iowa into a marvel of agricultural production. Daily, we see the fruits of their labor in our grain handling and processing industries, in our farm equipment manufacturers, in our feed and seed and

prairie settlers who kept the grass short around their log cabins to reduce the hazards of wildfires and rattlesnakes. We also plant trees, just like those early farmers who tried to temper the prairie gales and the blazing sun with windbreaks and shady groves that still dot the countryside.

We've forged our union with the land diligently, over the decades. Indian farmers first tilled small fields and gardens, growing corn and other crops. And the state's first Euro-American settlers, hardy German and Norwegian and Dutch and Scots-Irish immigrants, came mostly for the fertile soil.

Canada geese rest on open water at Rice Lake in Winnebago County.

Photos on pages 4–5 by Lowell Washburn

Oak-hickory woods are common today across much of southern Iowa. (Shimek State Forest, Lee County)

John Walkowiak

Constance Tuthill

Iowa's climate supported a vast native prairie prior to Euro-American settlement. Lavender spikes of blazing star, white balls of rattlesnake master, and golden rays of black-eyed Susan bloom in August at Williams Prairie State Preserve in Johnson County.

chemical businesses, and in our section-line roads dividing square croplands.

But most Iowans cling to another legacy as well. Instinctively, we're drawn to the shade of a bur oak, a gnarled veteran that survived long-ago prairie fires only to be caught up in the ceaseless battle between woodland and prairie. We pile bird-seed on our windowsills, reaching out to the creatures whose homes and habitat we may have disrupted in our attempt to harness the land. Picnickers and swimmers and boaters and anglers crowd close to our precious lakes and rivers. We prize our woodland trees – some for their beauty, some for their lumber, some for the solitude we find beneath their canopies. With childlike wonder, we delight in the grace of a monarch butterfly, the intricacy of a spiderweb, the promise of a north-bound flock of geese, the aroma of a wild rose, and the antics of a fox squirrel.

A monarch butterfly rests in a cluster of blazing star at Cayler Prairie State Preserve in Dickinson County.

Daryl Howell

The question is not what you look at, but what you see.
– Henry David Thoreau, Walden, 1854

We name our rivers, streets, subdivisions, shopping malls, truck stops, sports teams, and even pesticides for the plants and animals and people that make up our natural and cultural heritage. Some of us fish or hunt or trap because we feel a tie to ancestors who lived off the land. To some, it feels good to till a garden or grow flowers or plant trees.

More than 100 centuries, 10,000-plus years of time and cultural transition, separate us from the mastodon hunters. To be sure, the land has changed, and we, in turn, have left our indelible stamp upon the land. No, we cannot relive the times or recreate the places those prehistoric humans knew. Yet, in the ways of the Earth, their footprints have barely faded. In geologic time, we're only a heartbeat removed from people whose Iowa roots we share. We live on the same land, gaze over the same valleys, and bond to the same rich earth.

As you read this story of Iowa's land, reflect on those connections to the natural world, to the larger circle of life, and to the deeper rhythms of the Earth. Take time to get better acquainted with our land community and its many citizens – be they plant, animal, human, rock, soil, air, or water.

Each citizen is a thread in the fabric of the canvas on which our land's portrait is painted. But only we, as human beings, can choose the tints and textures and brush-strokes to bring that portrait to life. For our children's sake, we must not take those choices lightly.

Coyote

People Meet the Land

Wild turkey

Columbine

ANCIENT PEOPLES: THE FIRST IOWANS – From Siberia, nomadic people crossed into North America perhaps 15,000 years ago, no doubt following herds of caribou, musk oxen, and mammoths. They traversed a land bridge exposed when expanses of glacial ice had captured enough seawater to lower the ocean level. By 13,000 years ago, those Paleo-Indian people had found their way to Iowa, where they lived in what must have been harsh conditions alongside the remnants of glaciers. The warming climate eventually halted the glacial advances, however, and plants and animals quickly reoccupied the damp, dark, stony soils that formed on top of and at the edges of the decaying ice.

Those early Iowans moved about in cool, moist, spruce and fir forests interspersed with open meadows and wetlands. Hunters pursued mastodons, giant bison, and other big game, often working together to drive the animals over cliffs or into boggy mires where the prey could be attacked more easily. The Indians killed and butchered their quarry with effective stone spears and sharp tools painstakingly crafted from flint. People's lives were short, and populations were sparse – perhaps never reaching more than a few hundred at any one time.

As the climate continued to warm about 10,000 to 8,000 years ago, more hardwood forests grew up, with prairies gradually pushing in from the south and west. Ancient Iowans followed the resources, camping near rivers to gather wild plants and hunt small game and often traveling to hunt bison. But the innovative native people also began using the atlatl, or

This glacial scene resembles the wasting ice sheet present in north-central Iowa 13,500 to 12,000 years ago. The meltwater lake and its bordering coniferous trees are perched on the surface of glacial debris still underlain by whitish layers of ice. (Klutlan Glacier, Yukon Territory, Canada)

H. E. Wright Jr.

8

spear thrower, to increase their hunting efficiency. They learned to grind and chip stone into tools, such as axes, knives, scrapers, and plant-milling devices. Evidence at numerous archaeological sites suggests that populations were growing, perhaps into the thousands.

From about 2,800 to 800 years ago, prehistoric Woodland Indians inhabited an Iowa landscape much like that visited by the first European explorers. Eastern forests met western prairies, with scattered trees on the savanna in between. The trees and shrubs marched out into the grasslands during wet cycles, then retreated to the valleys during droughts. Native Americans also set fires to kill the woody plants and improve prairie wildlife habitat.

The Woodland people are noted for their use of cultivated plants. The Indians grew corn, beans, squash, sunflowers, tobacco, marsh elder, goosefoot, and other crops to supplement their diet of wild game and plants. Bison remained a staple food in western Iowa. The animals' hides were used for clothing and shelter, and their bones served as tools. During the Woodland period, people used bows and arrows, made a variety of styles of pottery, and traded with other Indians across the Midwest. The population in what would become Iowa grew to an estimated 10,000 people.

The best-known legacy of the Woodland people may be their intriguing mounds of earth. The earliest conical mounds apparently were for burials, but these and later mounds also may have served ceremonial functions. Effigy Mounds National

Jean C. Prior

Indian burial mounds were built on high bluffs or on terraces overlooking river valleys. The mounds also may have marked hunting territories, served as ceremonial centers, or embodied spiritual links with the earth. (Fish Farm Mounds State Preserve, Allamakee County)

R. Clark Mallam

Great bird mounds take clear shape when outlined with lime as part of a special study done in the 1970s. Iowa's effigy mounds represent creatures from the land, water, and sky. "The mounds and their builders have a message for us today – the human race must integrate itself with the rest of the living world." – R. Clark Mallam, 1986.

Monument, near Marquette, protects nearly 200 mounds, including several in the form of bear or bird effigies built between 450 B.C. and A.D. 1300.

Native American populations in Iowa grew to tens of thousands by about A.D. 1600, but then numbers dropped, apparently due to deaths from warfare and the spread of European diseases. Before the population decline, however, large villages thrived in several parts of Iowa. One encampment ranged across the Big Sioux River valley at Blood Run in northwestern Iowa and southeastern South Dakota. Some communities included elaborate earth lodges, palisade fortifications, large storage pits, and longhouses.

Many other Indian cultures also left physical remnants of their life in Iowa. Archaeological sites throughout the state include campsites, villages, quarries, workshops, rock carvings, mounds, and cemeteries.

1673: MARQUETTE AND JOLIET – When Iowans stand at one of our favorite spots, the overlook at Pike's Peak State Park south of McGregor, we see more than just a scenic vista. From that limestone blufftop, we can look back more than three centuries through history.

Just below lies the legendary Mississippi River, which drains the heartland of the nation, cradles cities, supports industries, carries twenty-first century commerce, delights recreationists, and nurtures fish and wildlife. From the east, flowing out of a wide valley to be swallowed up by the even-wider Mississippi, comes the Wisconsin.

On a misty morning, when the floodplain trees fade in and out of the fog, it's easy to picture that scene more than 300 years ago when Ioway Indians may have watched some of the first Europeans to visit Iowa. Explorer and fur trader Louis Joliet, along with missionary and Jesuit priest Father Jacques Marquette, paddled down the Wisconsin River, then entered the Mississippi on June 17, 1673. Sent by the Canadian governor to search for a route to the Pacific Ocean, they had begun at the Straits of Mackinac, then paddled across Lake Michigan, through Green Bay, and up the Fox River. After portaging overland to the Wisconsin River, they headed downstream to the Mississippi, where they found an imposing promontory we now know as Pike's Peak.

His party reached the Mississippi "with a joy I cannot express," Father Marquette later recalled. But his group of seven adventurers apparently did not go ashore in what is now Iowa. Several days later, on June 25, they landed south of present-day Keokuk, at the mouth of the Des Moines River. There they visited a village of Peoria Indians, who gave them a peace pipe and sent along the chief's ten-year-old son as a guide.

The contact between Marquette and Joliet and the Indians marked a milestone in a long period of interaction between the two cultures and the beginning of massive changes in Indian ways of life. The Europeans sought lead and furs, as well as access to the native people's lands. The Native Americans wanted the newcomers' metal tools, guns, and cloth. In

Stone axes (top) and celts (bottom two) were attached to wooden or bone handles and used to break firewood, smash large bones, and girdle trees.

Havana pottery is noted for toothed designs and geometric patterns pressed into the clay vessels. (Middle Woodland period, ca. A.D. 1.)

Projectile points found in Iowa (Clovis, above; Snyders, below) were chipped from flint (chert), a form of silica found in sedimentary rocks.

A rare copper celt from southeastern Iowa probably was used for ceremonial purposes.

Petroglyphs of the thunderbird, a spirit figure, are etched into rock faces across the upper Midwest.

This necklace made of bear claws is a type of adornment often worn by warriors and other men of high status.

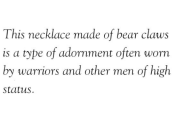

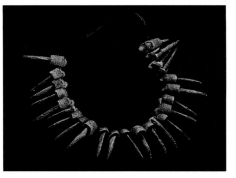

Ceremonial and religious objects were made from a variety of earthen materials. This finely carved claystone platform pipe, dating to ca. A.D. 100, is a bird effigy from southeast Iowa.

This eastern Iowa platform pipe was carved of aragonite, a cave mineral from southern Indiana, ca. A.D. 100.

Protective, overhanging ledges along valley walls (rock shelters) were frequently inhabited by Native Americans. (Wildcat Den State Park, Muscatine County)

Axe and celt photos by Iowa Dept. of Natural Resources; all other photos by Office of the State Archaeologist

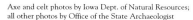

11

This panoramic view shows the historic entry of Marquette and Joliet (in two canoes) into the Upper Mississippi Valley via the Wisconsin River on June 17, 1673. Visitors to Pike's Peak State Park in Clayton County can see the same magnificent view today. This diorama is the centerpiece of Iowa Hall at the University of Iowa Museum of Natural History.

the bargain, the Indians also got disease, alcohol, and the eventual loss of their land.

Marquette and Joliet barely touched the west bank of the Mississippi, just enough perhaps, to marvel at the abundant wildlife, forested bluffs, hilltop prairies and savannas, and diverse vegetation along the tributaries. Other Europeans would explore across what is now Iowa in the next 150 years.

In the Mississippi Valley itself, French voyageurs probably had begun mining lead and trapping animals for fur by the mid-1600s. In 1788, Julien Dubuque struck a deal with the Meskwakis to mine lead along the Mississippi River at the mouth of Catfish Creek near the city that would bear his name. By 1800, the Meskwakis asserted property rights over the Iowa River valley, but they were pressured into giving up parts of that land in 1804, 1832, 1836, 1837, and 1842 – each time moving farther up the river. They finally called a halt to the displacements in the 1850s, when tribal members still in Iowa and those who'd been moved to western reservations joined together to buy their own land in Tama County.

As contacts with Europeans increased in the early to mid-1700s, Indian cultures were changed. The Ioway and Oto moved west and south, pushed by colonial expansion and by the Sauk, Meskwaki, Ho-Chunk, and other people from the Great Lakes region.

1804: LEWIS AND CLARK – The Louisiana Purchase of 1803 was followed the next year by Lewis and Clark's "Voyage of Discovery" up the Missouri River along what would become Iowa's western border. Although European traders, trappers,

up & Down as I Can See." The short prairie grasses, predominantly little bluestem, made the hills look bare. "This prarie I call Bald pated Prarie," Clark wrote, suggesting emptiness. But the party later went hunting along a stream the Indians called "Neesh-nah-ba-to-na" (today's Nishnabotna River) and found the region far from barren. They killed four deer, and saw "oake, walnut & mulberry" trees.

All along the Iowa border, the explorers marveled at the bounty of wildlife in the valley. The hunters sometimes killed as many as five deer a day. The travelers caught their first channel catfish near present-day Council Bluffs, where they found the creatures "verry Common and easy taken." Around Onawa, Lewis didn't even try to count the number of pelicans, except to exclaim that their numbers "appear almost in credible." Near

and explorers already had been prowling the land for years, the Louisiana Purchase marked the "official" beginning of Iowa's connection to the new nation that was emerging on the North American continent.

In stark contrast to the Mississippi River forests in eastern Iowa, trees were scarce along the Missouri River valley. At a site near the present Iowa-Missouri border, Clark described today's Loess Hills as "a range of Ball [bald] Hills parrelel to the river & at from 3 to 6 miles distant from it, and extends as far

Metal crosses and tokens were traded by Europeans to American Indians. These specimens were found near Dubuque, an early fur-trading and lead-mining center.

BELLEVUE AGENCY
Painting by Karl Bodmer

Bellevue is a few miles above the mouth of the Platte River, near the present-day site of Omaha, Nebraska. Here, Major John Dougherty maintained a government agency for the Oto, Pawnee, and Omaha tribes. Arriving on May 3, 1833, Prince Maximilian described it as "quite prettily situated on a hilltop,. . . . Below on the water lie a few huts, on the summit the agency building, the dwelling of a blacksmith and his family, and still more buildings."

WAHKTAGELI, YANKTON SIOUX CHIEF
Painting by Karl Bodmer

Wahktageli was about sixty years old when he posed for Bodmer on May 26, 1833, at Fort Lookout, the Sioux Agency near present-day Pierre, South Dakota. He paused now and then to smoke the pipe-tomahawk that he holds in his hand. His moccasins, leggings, and shirt are embroidered with brightly dyed porcupine quills. In his ears are strings of blue glass beads, and his face is painted with vermillion.

We Indians respect our ancestors. They are present in our ceremonies and we call upon them for help to live our lives.
– Maria Pearson, Yankton Sioux, Ames, Iowa, 1983

Sioux City, Clark commented on "verry plentiful" beaver, "verry fat ducks," and plovers "of different Kinds."

The valley had become lush and productive since the last floods of glacial meltwater receded 10,000 years before. The Missouri River had settled down to a more stable pattern of high water in the spring, low flows in the summer and fall, and periodic wanderings across the wide flats. Over the centuries, the restless river cut new channels, left oxbows, created wetlands, built sandbars, toppled shoreline trees, and deposited layers of silt. Native Americans were drawn to the region to hunt, fish, and raise crops. This was the Missouri River that Lewis and Clark's party explored, and the valley that beckoned to pioneers pushing west across the continent.

WAKUSASSE, FOX MAN
Painting by Karl Bodmer

The inscription on this portrait identifies the subject as Wakusasse, a Meskwaki (Fox) Indian. He wears a deer hair roach on his head, partially dyed with vermillion and ornamented with a feather, as a mark of success in battle. He also wears numerous shell or metal drop earrings, a blanket, and a necklace of beads.

NODAWAY ISLAND
Painting by Karl Bodmer

The steamboat Yellowstone, which carried Prince Maximilian's expedition up the Missouri River, reached the mouth of the Nodaway River on April 25, 1833. Woodcutters landed to obtain a supply of fuel, and Bodmer and Maximilian went ashore to gather botanical specimens. In the forest, they discovered a pair of abandoned frame shelters that Maximilian thought were made by the Sauks or Ioways.

Bodmer paintings courtesy of the Joslyn Art Museum, Omaha, Nebraska; Gift of Enron Art Foundation

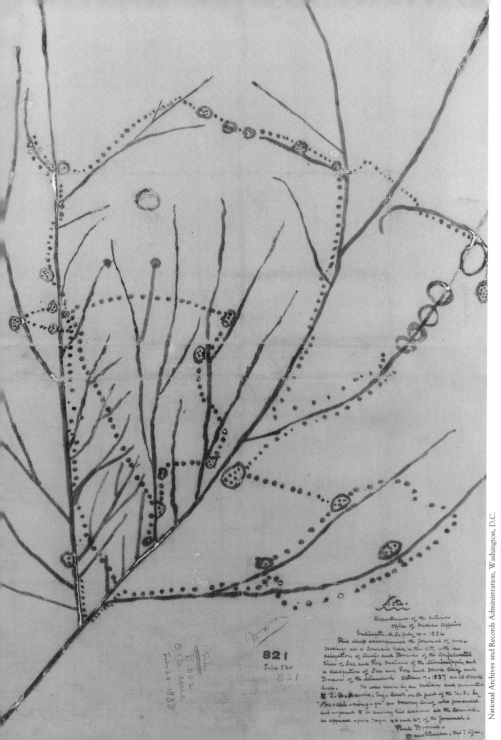

National Archives and Records Administration, Washington, D.C.

This is the route of my forefathers. It is the lands that we have always claimed from old times. We have the history. We have always owned this land. It is what bears our name.
– No Heart, Ioway Tribe, October 7, 1837

On October 7, 1837, No Heart and Moving Rain illustrated their Ioway land claims case before the Indian Commissioner in Washington, D.C., using this map drawn in charcoal. The Mississippi River flows from top center to the lower left corner. The map includes nearly sixty rivers and lakes, and extends from Lake Michigan on the east to the Niobrara and North Platte rivers on the west, and from southern Minnesota and Wisconsin on the north to the junction of the Missouri and Mississippi on the south. Portrayed are twenty-three village locations and the routes of movement between them. It is a remarkable map of historical memory, recording Ioway places throughout Iowa and surrounding states and events from 1830 back to the 1600s. (William Green, State Archaeologist of Iowa)

When I am here, the spirits of our ancestors are all around me.
– Pete Fee, Ioway Tribe, New Albin, Iowa, September 15, 1999

Geologists are piecing together Iowa's Ice Age history, and archaeologists teach us about the 600 generations of people who were here before Europeans arrived. But the explorers of the 1700s and 1800s not only made history, they began to record it. Two colorful adventurers, German Prince Maximilian du Wied and Swiss painter Karl Bodmer, traveled the Missouri River in 1832 and 1833, gathering data for an account of America's land and its people. Bodmer's meticulous watercolors and Maximilian's scientific observations of natural and cultural history give us rich insights into this period.

In 1805, Zebulon Pike led a military exploration to the Mississippi Valley, where he suggested building a fort on a bluff near what is now McGregor. Pike's Peak is now a state park, although the proposed fort was built across the river in Wisconsin. Downstream along the Mississippi, in 1808, Fort Madison became a military outpost that eventually led to the territory being opened for non-Indian settlement.

Iowa was poised on the brink of change. Native Americans, who had harvested the fish and wildlife, farmed, quarried, built, and traded throughout the region, were about to be displaced. The Indian people had lived on and worked the land for 3,000 years. Yet they sketched their legacy lightly on the landscape. Soon their subtle portraits would be painted over by the heavier hands – and greater numbers – of explorers and settlers. The new "artists" looked at the earth differently than the native peoples had, and the newcomers would change that landscape forever.

State Historical Society of Iowa, Iowa City

Fort Atkinson was a military post built between 1840 and 1842 to enforce the removal of the Winnebago (Ho-Chunk) Indians from Wisconsin into the Neutral Ground in Iowa. Then, in 1848, the Winnebago were removed from Iowa, and the last company of infantry left the fort in February 1849. Lt. A. W. Reynolds sketched this scene in 1843.

Michigan lily

Prairie racerunner

A Century of Change: 1800 to 1900

In the 1800s, Iowans reworked the face of their new state with a speed and to an extent perhaps unparalleled in human history. At the beginning of the century, a blanket of prairie cloaked three-quarters of this "land between two rivers." Pothole marshes dotted the flatter north-central part of the state, while a network of streams laced the rolling hills elsewhere across Iowa. Dense forests engulfed some valleys in the east and south, and groves of bur oaks climbed out of the river corridors and onto the ridges to form savannas. Thousands of Native Americans lived on the land, harvesting wild plants and animals, growing crops, and occasionally managing the vegetation with fire. By 1900, however, Euro-American settlers had claimed nearly all of Iowa's 36 million acres as farmland.

Non-Indian settlement officially began on June 1, 1833, when pioneers first were allowed to claim new land in the 6-million-acre Black Hawk Purchase along the west side of the Mississippi River. By 1846, when Iowa became a state, census records listed 96,088 people. The population doubled to 192,914 by 1850 and topped one million before 1870. In 1900, Iowa had 2.2 million people, compared to 2.9 million people today. Most lived on the state's 200,000 farms, working land where 95 percent of the prairie, two-thirds of the woodlands,

Rochester Cemetery, in Cedar County, is one of the Midwest's botanical showplaces. Historic gravestones nestle in the largest remnant of prairie remaining in the county. Scattered large oaks and hills of dune-sand add to the site's natural history.

Photographic Services, University of Iowa

and most of the wetlands had been converted to agriculture.

The earlier settlers may have preferred to stay close to forest edges, where they could cut trees for building materials, fences, and fuel. But the lack of trees on the expanses of prairie only briefly delayed the rush of settlement to the more open lands of northwest Iowa. Especially after the Civil War, there was a major push onto the prairies. And once the farmers came to an area, it took less than ten years for the "frontier" to become agricultural land.

Most of the prairie sod was turned under with oxen and breaking plows and later with steel plows. The remainder disappeared in the face of heavy grazing and competition from introduced grasses. Farmers also suppressed fires, which once had discouraged woody plants and alien species from invading the prairies. The few prairie remnants that survived often were wet areas that had been used to harvest wild hay. Many of those sites later would be doomed by dredges and tiling machines that made drainage easier, and also by continuing pressure in the twentieth century to cultivate more land.

The dramatic, swift, almost complete change of diverse prairie to a monoculture of cropland profoundly altered the ecosystem. Twenty-eight million acres of bluestem, dropseed, compass plants, coneflowers, gentians, and 200 other species were transformed, in a relative eyeblink, into a patchwork of corn, wheat, oats, hay, and pasture. Those plots have expanded to the huge roadside-to-roadside corn and soybean fields that we see today.

Courtesy of the Deere Art Collection, Moline, Illinois

In his painting Fall Plowing, *renowned Iowa artist Grant Wood focused on the geometric patterns that cultivation brought to the land, and he highlighted the implement of change – the plow. Wood captured the steeply rolling hills of southern and eastern Iowa farmland.*

At the same time, although to a lesser degree, the loss of forests also reshaped the state's landscape. Naturalist Bohumil Shimek described Iowa's pre-settlement forests: "There were still miles upon miles of almost undisturbed timber, fine white oaks predominating on the uplands, the hard maple occasionally dominating the river bluffs, and the red cedar finding an anchorage on the limestone ledges, while the black walnut and various softwood trees occupied the narrow bottom lands. The

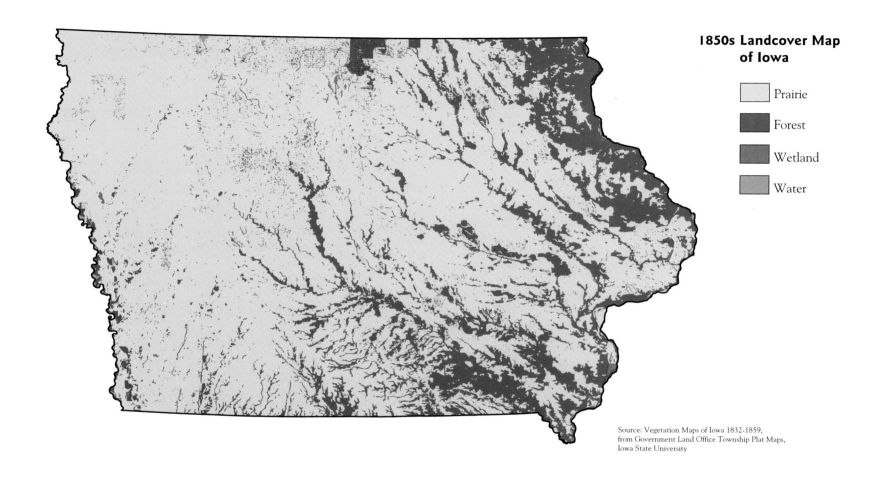

Source: Vegetation Maps of Iowa 1832-1859,
from Government Land Office Township Plat Maps,
Iowa State University

upland woods were carpeted in early spring with hepaticas and the rue anemone, while the ravines were decked with beautiful ferns, interspersed with pink and yellow ladies'-slippers and many other wild flowers, all in great profusion."

Early surveyors' notes suggested that trees covered about 6.7 million acres or 19 percent of Iowa around the time of statehood in 1846. Settlers steadily cleared the forests, however, as they grubbed out trees for cropfields, rail fences, log

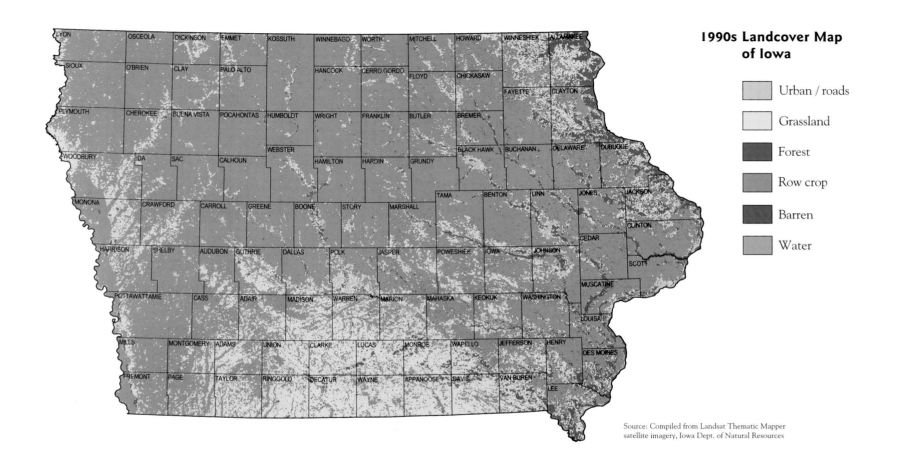

Source: Compiled from Landsat Thematic Mapper
satellite imagery, Iowa Dept. of Natural Resources

1990s Landcover Map of Iowa

- Urban / roads
- Grassland
- Forest
- Row crop
- Barren
- Water

buildings, and lumber. By 1857, the Iowa State Agricultural Society had issued a plea calling for more careful use of timber resources. Steamboat crews, who regularly stopped to cut trees to burn for fuel, decimated some forests along major rivers.

Maps above: The dramatic, swift, almost complete change of diverse prairie to a monoculture of cropland profoundly altered the native ecosystem.

Boat decks were stacked with cordwood. When railroads came to Iowa in 1855, they brought another assault on the woodlands. The state's eventual 10,000 miles of rail lines needed about six acres of oak woods, perhaps 800 trees, to make ties for every mile of track. What's more, those ties usually had to be replaced every five to seven years. Railroad cars, trestles, and fuel for some steam engines also required wood from the forests.

Often, trees grew back rapidly after they were cut. But with the invention of barbed wire in 1873, the forests faced another threat, as farmers found it easier to use woodlands for grazing. Although the livestock didn't always destroy the forests, the animals compacted the soil, ate or trampled seedlings, and changed the character of the woodland community. Coal mining also took its toll on forests as trees were cut to shore up mine shafts. By 1900, more than 4 million acres of Iowa's original forests had been lost to other uses.

As much as they cut trees, however, nineteenth-century Iowans liked to plant them. Many farmers started windbreaks and shelterbelts around their farmsteads for shade and protection from the prairie winds. As people controlled wildfires, and with roads and fields as firebreaks, tree growth expanded into what once had been grasslands. When cities grew, urban

Left: Riverboats carried settlers into the country's interior. The steamboats burned enormous amounts of wood, cut from the timber along Iowa's river valleys. This image was printed from an engraving on lithographic limestone quarried in Floyd County and published in Clement Webster's 1915 issue of Contributions to Science *to illustrate the high quality of this Iowa stone for printing.*

Right: This remarkable 1850 New Map of Iowa *illustrates the wave of change moving across the state from east to west in the middle of the nineteenth century. The eastern counties are bustling with township lines, numerous settlements, stagecoach roads, named rivers and streams, and the state capital at Iowa City. The western counties are not as well known, and some of their names did not stick – Buncombe, Risley, Yell, and Fox. "Indian Territory" lies west of the Missouri River. Note "Ft. Clark" and "Ft. des Moines" and the "site of Monroe, the new capital" in Jasper County. The terrain of the "Coteau des Prairies," the high ground of pothole wetlands that track the route of the last glacier through the eastern Dakotas, is noted extending into north-central Iowa.*

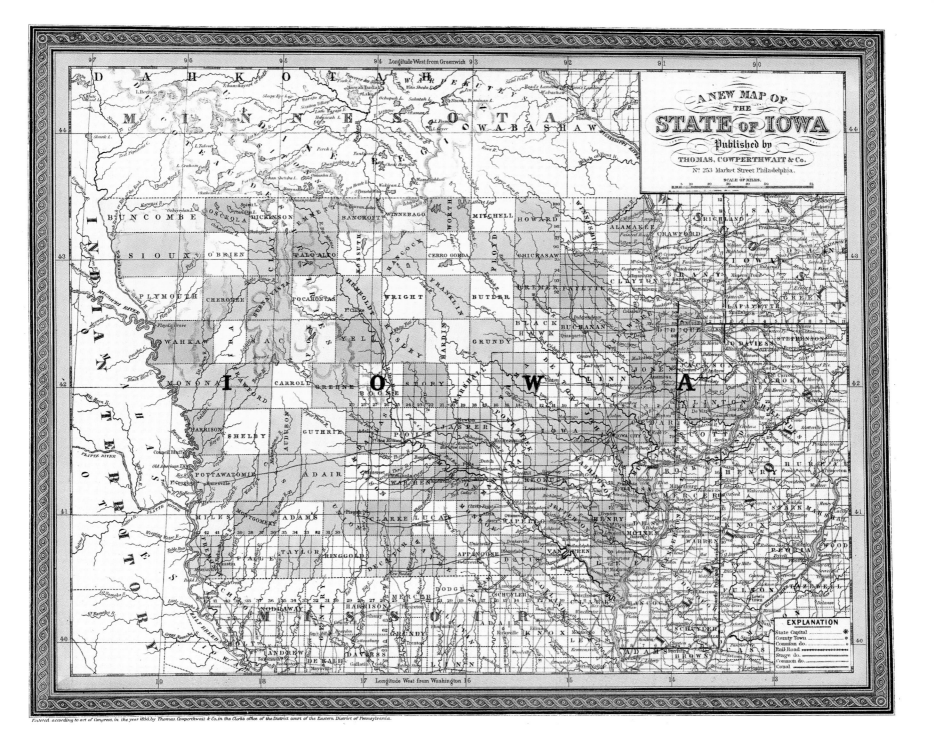

Gypsum was discovered in Iowa in the 1850s. Horse-drawn carts were used to haul slabs of gypsum from this quarry just south of Fort Dodge in 1902 for use as building stone and for mortar and plastering purposes, and later for the manufacture of wallboard.

residents also planted trees along streets, around houses, and in parks.

Still, Iowa was, and is, known more for its prairies than its trees. Especially in north-central and northwest Iowa, in the tracks of the most recent glaciers, a labyrinth of prairie marshes dotted the pre-settlement terrain. Ducks and geese, even trumpeter swans and whooping cranes, abounded in the wetlands. Muskrats, turtles, dragonflies, small fish, frogs, salamanders, marsh wrens, yellow-headed blackbirds, and other wildlife shared the potholes.

Beneath those waters full of abundant wildlife, however, lay some of the richest land on earth, a fact not lost on the pioneers who settled there. Farmers quickly tried to find ways to drain off the water so they could plant crops or harvest prairie hay. They first dug ditches by hand, then cut trenches with horse-drawn plows. Some fashioned wooden pipes, which later were replaced with clay tiles. By any means they could, the industrious farmers shuttled the water off their land to the nearest river or stream.

In the process, people transformed the sponge-like character of the land, where water once had soaked into the ground. The farmers' artificial drainage ditches began to expand, forming water courses that grew and eroded with more runoff. New tile lines diverted more water to the channels. Steam dredges cut drainage canals to further speed the water away. In place of flat land dappled with standing water, there developed a watershed with rivulets and creeks and streams

The Bealer Quarries in Cedar County, photographed here about 1900, were famous for their mechanization and output of stone for bridge piers and abutments. Many of Iowa's nineteenth-century bridges and buildings were built of limestone found outcropping along major rivers.

Photos on pages 24–25 from the Calvin Collection, University of Iowa

and rivers. Instead of seeping gradually into the land, the water was hurried away downstream through a new network of surface connections.

Elsewhere in Iowa, landowners often shortened or altered rivers. On the more rolling land, thousands of miles of rivers and streams had developed over thousands of years, as water found its way gradually downstream to the sea. If those sometimes-meandering rivers ran where people wanted to put farm fields or highways or other structures, engineers frequently used machines to straighten, or channelize, the waterways. The process started in the late 1800s but reached its peak in the early 1900s, after heavy equipment became more common. By some estimates, Iowa lost more than 3,000 miles of streams to channelization before government restrictions curtailed the practice. Channelization also sped the flow of floodwaters onto the land of downstream neighbors, lowered the water table, and encouraged the drainage of some lakes, sloughs, and river backwaters.

Even before Europeans began their nineteenth-century push to settle here, earlier miners had discovered some of Iowa's mineral resources. By the mid-1600s, French voyageurs and Native Americans were working lead mines along the Upper Mississippi River. Revolutionary War soldiers made bullets from lead mined at Dubuque. In 1788, Julien Dubuque settled in what is now Dubuque County near the mouth of Catfish Creek and negotiated mining rights with the Meskwaki.

25

This historic photograph shows a ledge of dolomite bedrock breaking the flow of the North Fork Maquoketa River at Cascade in Dubuque County. The natural outcrop forms the base for a low-head dam that supplied water power for the adjoining mill.

Lead and zinc mining would continue for more than a century, with the last mine closing in 1910.

Some of the state's earliest explorers were government geologists sent to assess the mineral resources. Although they may have been disappointed not to find tremendous mineral wealth, these scientists still made valuable observations on the state's natural resources and topography.

One discovery that did bring major changes was coal. Federal survey crews first reported coal deposits along the Mississippi River in 1835. Settlers began digging shallow "dog holes" to mine coal for home use, and by 1840, a few miners were extracting coal to sell. Steamboats occasionally burned coal, but it was the railroads that spurred the demand for coal in the late 1800s, as tracks pushed across the state and the country. For a time, Iowa was the last stop where the coal-burning locomotives could load a supply of fuel for the trip west. From 1874 until 1900, Iowa produced more coal than any other state.

Especially in south-central Iowa, some strip pits left moonscapes of barren tailings and water-filled excavations where miners had dug out the coal from just below the surface. Another 6,000 abandoned underground mines lie beneath about 80,000 acres of land at several sites. Some of the old mines occasionally still collapse, leaving craters and damaging property. Several old mine shafts lie just east of the Iowa Statehouse, in Des Moines.

As the push to develop the state accelerated, people

In 1886, an unexpected gush of water, known as Jumbo, flowed out of control for months during well drilling at Belle Plaine in Benton County. There is a continuing need to locate adequate sources of good-quality groundwater throughout Iowa.

quickly learned that Iowa's bedrock often makes good building material. From the Old Capitol, built of limestone in the territorial capital of Iowa City in 1840, to the Iowa Men's Reformatory, constructed in Anamosa starting in 1872, many stone buildings have become landmarks. The building-stone quarries were concentrated in eastern Iowa, but an outcrop of Iowa's oldest exposed bedrock, the Sioux Quartzite, at the far northwest tip of Iowa, has been used in a number of buildings in that region.

With the constant need for more building materials, manufacturers of clay product also sprang up across Iowa. By 1900, 381 companies were making bricks, drainage tile, and sewer tile. The turn-of-the-century push to drain and farm wetlands would make Iowa the leading producer of drainage tile by 1920.

Draining the wetlands, plowing the prairie, clearing the forests, and mining the land also destroyed or significantly altered the habitat for wildlife that once lived there. Our wildlife populations declined dramatically through the nineteenth century. The first white explorers marveled at the bison, elk, wild turkeys, deer, prairie chickens, bears, wolves,

Photos on pages 26–27 from the Calvin Collection, University of Iowa

Structures that housed underground coal mining operations were familiar scenes in south-central Iowa at the close of the nineteenth century when mining activity was near its peak. Coal fueled the expansion of railroads, industry, and home heating. The mining industry also attracted many immigrants to Iowa from other countries and states. Pictured here is the Consolidation Mine No. 8 near the former town of Givin in Mahaska County.

waterfowl, shorebirds, and other birds and animals that thrived in the fertile prairies and scattered woodlands. "I had never rode through a country so full of game," declared Joseph Street, an Indian agent who traversed the Turkey, Wapsipinicon, and Cedar rivers in northeast Iowa with a survey party in 1833.

The first non-Indian settlers killed game almost at will. They easily took deer, turkeys, and prairie chickens for food. In wetlands, people gathered duck, goose, and swan eggs in the spring and shot the birds virtually year-round for food and feathers. Market hunters also slaughtered shorebirds and waterfowl by the hundreds, often shipping the birds to restaurants in eastern cities.

River otters and beavers initially thrived in most rivers, streams, and marshes, and trappers sought them for fur during the heyday of the fur trade in the late 1700s. During the nineteenth century, trapping pressure, habitat loss, water

Kilns, sheds, and neat stacks of finished clay tiles are seen at the Iowa Pipe and Tile Company plant in Des Moines about 1896. The plant relied on outcrops of clay shale nearby along the Des Moines River. Miles of tile were used to drain the natural wetlands of north-central Iowa for agricultural use.

Photos on pages 28–29 from the Calvin Collection, University of Iowa

pollution, wetland drainage, and stream channelization gradually took their toll. Beavers and otters were essentially gone from Iowa around 1900.

The combination of hunting, a growing human population, and the conversion of prairies and forests and wetlands to farm fields spelled doom for many species. By 1867, the last Iowa mountain lion had been killed. Bison vanished from the state in 1870, elk in 1871, black bears in 1876, wolves about 1885, and whooping cranes by 1894. Passenger pigeons were mostly gone from Iowa by the 1890s, and they would become extinct by 1914.

It was a time of transition. In the nineteenth century, we changed our state from a place controlled by natural forces to a landscape dominated by human handiwork. A pioneer child might have ridden in a covered wagon on a trackless prairie, watching elk and prairie chickens. That same person could have greeted the twentieth century with a ride behind a steam locomotive, on tracks linking urban industrial centers, passing neat farmsteads built on a mile-square grid of roads.

Incredibly, this astounding transformation from a natural landscape of wild places teeming with wild creatures to a checkerboard of manicured cropfields, cities, and roads, took place in barely sixty to seventy years, less than a lifetime.

Calls for Conservation

Little bluestem

Blue-eyed grass

Barn owl

By the end of the nineteenth century, Iowans no longer could ignore the destruction that had accompanied our first fifty years of statehood. In the process of building a strong farm economy, stable industries, growing cities, and an efficient transportation system, we also had ravaged many of the natural features and resources of the land. Visionary leaders began to call for protecting some of the remaining natural heritage.

Thomas Macbride, a University of Iowa botany professor who also was president of the Iowa Academy of Science, a founder and president of the Iowa Parks and Forestry Association, and later, president of the University of Iowa, led the conservation movement.

In his 1902 president's address to the Parks and Forestry Association, Macbride described the losses of the state's natural beauty that he had witnessed in just his own fifty-four years: "... little of it [is] left for our injury or desecration; the prairies are plowed almost to the last acre; the woodlands have been cleared away entirely or converted into pasturelands ... ; the streams near the town are the dumping place for all un-

cleanness and in the country are esteemed only as a convenient place for watering domestic animals."

Macbride continued his pleas to establish parks and to protect watersheds and forests, pleas that he had initiated in addresses to the Academy of Science in 1895 and 1897. The Academy also had petitioned the Iowa Legislature in 1896, but to no avail, asking for laws to help protect the state's natural lakes. He also urged Iowans to recognize their "environmental rights" to clean air and natural beauty: "Is it not possible for us as intelligent self-governing people ... to use wealth and opportunity and power in such wise [ways] as to conserve for

The people would act today if the situation were clearly understood. The question is whether we do the right thing now or wait until the expense shall have increased a hundredfold.
– Thomas H. Macbride, President's address to the Iowa Academy of Science, 1897

IOWA'S EARLY CONSERVATION LEADERS

Office of the State Archaeologist

Bohumil Shimek
Ecologist

Special Collections, University of Iowa Libraries

Ellison Orr
Archaeologist

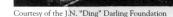

Ada Hayden
Botanist (left)

J. N. "Ding" Darling
Cartoonist

Courtesy of the J.N. "Ding" Darling Foundation

Botany Dept., Iowa State University

Thomas Macbride
Natural scientist

Macbride and Calvin photos from the Calvin Collection, University of Iowa

Louis Pammel
Biologist

Samuel Calvin
Geologist

Special Collections, Iowa State University Library

Calvin Collection, University of Iowa

Backbone State Park, dedicated in 1920, was the first in Iowa's park system. This scenic treasure in Delaware County provides recreation, education, and inspiration for young and old alike. Ledges and crevices of weathered dolomite at "The Backbone" provide the backdrop for this family outing in the late 1890s.

ourselves and our children all those finer instincts of humanity?"

Laws might be needed to bring out those "finer instincts," Macbride acknowledged. It should be "a criminal offense . . . to allow any species of filth, from hog-lots, barnyards, privies, dead animals, or anything of the sort to drain into or find exit in the waters of any lake or stream," he said. Pressure from Macbride and others led the legislature to strengthen the powers of the State Board of Health in 1913.

Still, Macbride firmly believed in conservation as wise use, rather than strict preservation. "Our streams are for use," he said. "Conservation bids us to use them and use them wisely; likewise our forests, these shall not simply stand as in the ages primeval, they must stand and be productive, be used."

Along with Iowa State College botanist Louis H. Pammel, Macbride worked to establish a system of state parks in Iowa. Their efforts led to the establishment of the State Board of Conservation in 1917 and eventually to the dedication of Iowa's first state park, Backbone, near Strawberry Point, in

1920. Although Macbride might have quarreled with the idea of recreational "multiple use" in parks that he had conceived as natural areas, he recognized the need for all people to have places to go to get in touch with the land and with nature. "The park shall set us free," Macbride said.

Despite the success of the park advocates, however, many Iowans argued that the state's natural treasures remained in danger. They realized that many of our original resources had been permanently lost or altered and that the state was on the verge of sacrificing much, much more.

In 1931, the Iowa General Assembly instructed the State Board of Conservation (the parks agency) and the State Fish and Game Commission (which oversaw wildlife management) to prepare a twenty-five year conservation plan. The charge was to lay out a blueprint for the "orderly and scientific development of natural resources, recreational areas and park systems of the whole state."

We must admire the commitment to conservation shown by the legislators and others who conceived the twenty-five year plan. With the farm economy suffering and much of the country sliding into the Great Depression, these people could have been tempted to deal only with short-term economic problems. Yet they recognized the significance of natural resources to the state's future and were willing to suggest an ambitious strategy for protecting Iowa's natural heritage.

At the forefront of the effort were such prominent Iowa conservationists as *Des Moines Register* cartoonist J. N. "Ding"

Civilian Conservation Corps workers built many beautiful and useful structures on public lands in Iowa. The shore patrol station (above) and rustic lodge at Gull Point State Park in Dickinson County are excellent examples. The rounded, colorful field stones left by glacial melting are abundant in the region and make good construction materials for buildings.

Darling; Margo Frankel of Des Moines, for whom Margo Frankel Woods State Park was named; J. G. Wyth of Cedar Falls, whose namesake is George Wyth State Park; and Ada Hayden, who advocated prairie protection and a system of state preserves. Among the many consultants on the project was native Iowan Aldo Leopold, the forester and wildlife

Courtesy of the J. N. "Ding" Darling Foundation

HERE COME THE NATURE LOVERS
J. N. "Ding" Darling, 1927

biologist who became famous for his later writings, including the conservation classic, *A Sand County Almanac.*

The conservation plan published in 1933, 100 years after Iowa was opened to settlement, bluntly listed the losses of the past century: "the waste of Iowa's greatest asset, the soil; the unwise destruction of surface waters by drainage, pollution and silting; the heedless stripping of woodlands; the almost wanton destruction of wild life; the irrational use of funds for recreation in several forms; the patent failure to capitalize the state's fine potentialities all along the line."

Rather than dwell on negatives, the plan spelled out details for work that would not only "call a halt" to the abuse, but also might rebuild the resource base for future generations. Decades later, we still must commend the extraordinary foresight of proposals to fight soil erosion, improve fish and wildlife habitat, build parks, preserve prairie, and beautify roadsides.

All told, the planners estimated the costs of the proposals, including land acquisition and improvements, at only $2 to $3 per person, or $9 to $12 per family. The cost could be paid by hunting and fishing license fees, park concessions, gasoline or automobile taxes, cigarette taxes, or special levies, the document said. Significantly, the plan also suggested legislation and governmental reorganization to benefit conservation.

Many of the plan's components came to pass, some sooner and some later. Iowa's county conservation board system, which was a model for many states, began with legislation

1933 Conservation Plan Highlights

✓ *Provide state aid to landowners to fight erosion.*

✓ *Clean up and provide access to state lakes and rivers.*

✓ *Help landowners with forest management. Set aside state forests.*

✓ *Restore wildlife with habitat improvement, research, and refuges. Help landowners and provide habitat along roadsides and other public lands.*

✓ *Make Iowa's fishing "better than it ever has been." Stop pollution, build artificial lakes, protect natural lakes and streams, and restock many waters.*

✓ *Establish a state park within forty miles of every Iowan, and set aside a network of at least seventy-five state preserves to protect unique natural areas.*

✓ *Integrate scenic highways and roadside parks into the conservation plan.*

✓ *Preserve remnants of Iowa's prairie, nearly gone in 1933.*

✓ *Combine Board of Conservation with Fish and Game Commission.*

✓ *Protect fishing and hunting license fees from diversion to other uses.*

✓ *Add easements for public access and to protect scenic areas.*

✓ *Restrict commercial use near state lakes, parks, and preserves.*

✓ *Give counties planning and zoning authority.*

✓ *Regulate timber cutting with zoning.*

✓ *Give counties authority to organize park districts.*

✓ *License billboards.*

✓ *Authorize Highway Commission to build roads in state parks.*

Courtesy of the J. N. "Ding" Darling Foundation

TIME TO TAKE AN INVENTORY OF OUR PANTRY
J. N. "Ding" Darling, 1936

Left: Started in 1909, Iowa Lakeside Laboratory on West Okoboji Lake is a legacy of Thomas Macbride and his colleagues Samuel Calvin and Bohumil Shimek, who believed this was an ideal location to teach Iowans about the state's natural beauty and the richness of its lake, forest, and prairie life. The facility today features historic buildings in a natural setting to create a unique learning environment for students and visitors. The handsome and durable Shimek Lab is constructed of colorful, rounded igneous and metamorphic boulders left throughout the area by glacial ice.

passed in 1955, some twenty-two years after the idea was formally proposed. The plan also launched construction of artificial lakes at dozens of sites, which now are key areas for fishing and recreation.

When the Fish and Game Commission and the Board of Conservation were combined into the Iowa Conservation Commission in 1935, the new agency was governed by a citizen commission that insulated the department from politics. The move was considered a model for other states.

"Ding" Darling's leadership also brought the first federal duck stamp to help pay for wetland protection in 1934, and the Cooperative Wildlife Research Units at Iowa State College and other state schools across the nation, beginning in 1932.

Some other ideas in the plan have changed considerably or become blurred through the years. For example, the plan's definition of a park, preserve, wildlife refuge, and sanctuary is not always clear today. We can agree, however, that "the state preserve and state park offer the best opportunity for the over-wrought mind to recapture its serenity and dignity and spiritual power." The 1933 plan emphasized the need for roadside

Right: This beautiful stone bridge spans Wesley Creek at Lacey-Keosauqua State Park in Van Buren County. Civilian Conservation Corps crews hand-quarried blocks of limestone from nearby outcrops to build this and other structures within the park. The historic quarry, while overgrown, is still accessible by foot.

management, but it's taken decades for us to recognize the potential of highway corridors as refuges for wildlife and native plants. Statewide zoning – of everything from billboards to timber cutting – did not catch on. County zoning in many cases drew a similar negative response. And the concept of protecting the land or natural features by easements has not gained popularity, as the 1933 planners had hoped it might.

Still, the plan became a catalyst for conservation. Several groups, both public and private, that today lead Iowa's conservation movement can trace their roots to the dedication of those early leaders. The ambitious recommendations, presented nearly seven decades ago, set goals that shaped Iowa's conservation accomplishments for the rest of the twentieth century. And the authors laid down a challenge that may apply equally to the twenty-first century: "Let every citizen of Iowa catch and hold that vision of the economy and the enrichment of human living to be achieved only through state-wide, far-sighted development plans. Not for too visionary, but for too meager-minded planning shall we be held to account."

Photos on pages 36–37 by Robert McKay

Hickory hairstreak butterfly

Blazing star

Land: A Geologic Inheritance

Gray catbird

"Nature was in a most pleasant mood when our land was fashioned. She bounded us by two mighty rivers, here ever to be harnessed for power unlimited. She pencilled the landscape for beauty and utility. She left lake, and stream, and wooded hill, she gave forest and prairie for the pioneer, and coal to turn the wheels of industry. Life in abundance was hid in the soil, waiting only the hand of the plowman and springtime's gentle kiss to blossom into a harvest abundant to feed a hungry world."

Governor William L. Harding didn't try to hide his love of Iowa when he made his inaugural address on January 16, 1919. Like many Iowans, he gave in to the temptation to boast a little when talking about our land. But why shouldn't we acknowledge the earth? We draw our very life from it. The Indians who built the effigy mounds along the Mississippi Valley more than 1,000 years ago may have shaped those images to symbolize their own physical and mystical connections with the land, air, and water. The state's early immigrants were drawn here by the promise of fertile soil, abundant game, and good water supplies.

Gravity dictates that we touch the land, walk on it, return to it.

The land is our foundation. And that foundation sits on a deep geological inheritance that has been unfolding for eons. One individual usually can observe only small natural changes to the landscape in his or her lifetime. We may see a brief moment, a scratch on the surface, of that dynamic earth history. But if enough small events, and occasional larger ones, continue for a very long time, they can combine to literally transform the face of a continent.

Iowa's landscape, both visible and underground, still bears the signatures that tell the story of the geologic forces that shaped our state. We can study their bold, unmistakable inscriptions on the surface where we live. But if we read between the lines and interpret the footnotes, we also can understand the deeper, hidden layers of older, buried landscapes and seascapes. The ancient sea floors, coral reefs, shore lines, coastal swamps, tropical river systems, melting ice sheets, and wind-blown dust produced the earth materials that form the backbone of Iowa's land.

Today we work this land, or perhaps we should say the land works for us. It grows our food, supports our buildings, provides raw materials for our industries, absorbs our wastes,

FOSSILS OF IOWA

Solitary
horn coral

Gastropod (snail shell)

Crinoid (stemmed sea animal)

Trilobites
(sea floor
animals)

Colonial
corals

Fossil photos by
Iowa Dept. of Natural Resources

Brachiopod shells

Leaves of seed-fern
and trunk of scale-tree

Teeth of mastodon (left) and mammoth (right)

39

Photos by Gary Hightshoe, Iowa State University

Far left: The collapse of rock and soil into underground crevices and caves causes sinkholes (circular pits) in regions of shallow limestone. (Clayton County)
Near left: Meander loops and oxbow lakes along the Iowa River in Tama County indicate porous floodplain materials and a shallow water table. Knowing the composition of Iowa's earth materials is essential to understanding the capacity of the land to transmit contaminants and to protect water supplies.

and stores our water supplies. Therefore, we need to understand what this ground beneath us is like – what holds it up, what gives it shape and texture, what finite resources lie within its depths, how vulnerable it is to contamination sources, and whether it can heal itself if we damage it. Armed with this basic geological information, we can begin to comprehend how much the land and its characteristics affect our daily lives. And we can let the land itself guide our sensible use of its many

resources and our quest for solutions to environmental problems.

Iowa's landscape itself attests to the underlying geology. A change in terrain usually indicates a geologic change beneath the ground. Most of what Iowans see – elevation, drainage, and soil composition – are the products of glacial activity. For example, in the southern half of the state, rolling hills stereotype Iowa to many cross-state travelers. These are the familiar

Habitats of Iowa's plant and animal communities are a result of differences in earth materials and geologic history. Right: Muskrats are at home in the glacial wetlands that dot north-central Iowa. (Bjorkboda Marsh, Hamilton County)

Roger Hill

Don Poggensee

Bob Howe

Above: The ridged hills of deep loess in western Iowa contain some of the state's best remaining tracts of native prairie. Left: The passage of cool, moist air through creviced dolomite bedrock in northeast Iowa forms rare habitats (algific slopes) for plants that normally grow much farther north. (Dubuque County)

scenes from Grant Wood paintings, with cropfields and pastures, farms and towns. How many people realize that glaciers set this pastoral scene more than 500,000 years ago? Erosion later carved deep valleys through the layers of pebbly clay, and wind-blown silt mantled the terrain. Sometimes, the valleys cut deep enough to reach bedrock, exposing coal seams and tropical plant fossils formed 400 million years ago, when the land was a maze of coastal swamps.

Prehistoric people lived and farmed along the streams and on the hilltops. Newly arrived settlers and their descendants tucked cities beside the rivers and built farmsteads on the uplands. Farm ponds and reservoirs, like Red Rock and

Rathbun, now supplement the region's scarce groundwater supplies. Despite the rolling terrain, careful farmers learned to protect the land. They trim their cropfields with terraces and

MINERALS OF IOWA

Geode
(State Rock)

Calcite
crystal

Agates

Pyrite
("fool's gold")

Copper
nugget

Stalactite of calcite

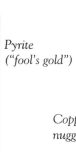

Gypsum

Sioux
Quartzite

Calcite
and pyrite

Coal

Galena
(lead ore)

Mineral photos by
Iowa Dept. of Natural Res

42

waterways, grow hay on the steeper slopes, raise cattle on the grasslands, and protect the oak-hickory forests. Without such vigilance, landowners might lose their topsoil to erosion and their woodlands to trampling by livestock.

Along the state's borders, two great rivers – the Missouri on the west and the Mississippi on the east – dominate the land and its geologic history.

The broad floodplain of the Missouri speaks of torrents of glacial meltwater. During summer months, from about 31,000 to 12,500 years ago, the floods spread for miles across the valley. In winters, the melting slowed and the waters receded to expose dried silt and mud. Fierce west winds whipped the fine deposits into the air, then piled the loess in thick blankets along the eastern side of the valley, eventually forming the Loess Hills. The windblown dust also spread eastward, falling in thinner layers across much of the rest of what now is Iowa. The process was copied, on a smaller scale, along many of the state's other rivers.

The Loess Hills sheltered Native Americans, who lived in the protected valleys, hunted on the open prairies, and fished in the rivers and oxbow lakes. Lewis and Clark marveled at the abundant wildlife of these hills two centuries ago. Pioneers brought cattle to graze on the native grasses and worked tirelessly to drain and plow the river bottoms. Later, in an effort to tame the floods along the Missouri and its tributaries, engineers straightened some streams and built levees to confine their flows.

If you had been looking for a very long, geologic time, you could have seen the continents themselves in motion, drifting apart on their crustal plates, held afloat by the fire beneath.
– Lewis Thomas, The Lives of a Cell, 1974

As human tampering sped the water along, the riverbeds cut deeper and banks eroded. Nearby wetlands dried up as their water seeped away through the sandy underground connections between the river and surrounding land. Still, the aquifers hold ample water to supply wells both for irrigation and for drinking water.

Despite changes in the Missouri River, the mystique of the Loess Hills endures. Unique in the western hemisphere, the Loess Hills lure a host of visitors: scientists studying unusual plant and animal life; families seeking home sites; developers marketing the scenery; contractors in search of fill dirt; and recreationists who want to hike or bike or camp or hunt along prairie ridges or secluded woody slopes. The unusual terrain and biological features of the region have prompted talk of national protection and further recognition.

An equally dramatic river valley rules our eastern border. But bedrock, rather than loose silt, dominates the Mississippi Valley. Outcrops of rock that formed on tropical seabeds 300 to 550 million years ago now define the Mississippi Valley and

Gary Hightshoe, Iowa State University

John M. Zielinski

Above: Ancient Iowans were drawn to places where the land speaks in scenic eloquence. (Turkey River Mounds State Preserve, Clayton County) Above right: An Amish farmer and his draft horses work the land together near Sharon Center in southern Johnson County.

dictate the sharp bends and narrow canyons of its tributaries. Some streams have cut deep channels into the rock during the 500,000 years since the region's last glacial encounter. Spectacular blufftop overlooks, hidden caves, springs, white-water creeks, and colorful fall leaves attract tourists. Numerous quarries tap the readily accessible limestone. One prominent rock outcrop, the Silurian Escarpment, winds from Iowa all the way to the east end of Lake Erie, where it cradles Niagara Falls.

But the same rock formations that shape the scenic topography of Iowa's "Little Switzerland" also mandate caution

Near right: Iowa's land is a rich mosaic of cropland, pasture, timber, and a long rural heritage. (Saints Peter and Paul Church in northeast Johnson County) Middle: Gentle slopes, extraordinarily productive soils, and timely rains enable a bountiful soybean harvest. Far right: The abundance of grain and pasture also favors livestock production, such as this inquisitive herd of sheep.

Drake Hokanson

Photos by Photographic Services, University of Iowa

in use of the land. Fractures, fissures, and sinkholes in the rock can channel surface water directly into valuable underground aquifers. A manure or chemical spill could pollute a trout stream, upset the delicate balance of the area's unique biological habitats, or permanently taint the drinking water of thousands of people.

In north-central Iowa, the terrain offers a whole new set of challenges and opportunities. Here, farmers praise the flat, black, productive soils, while naturalists tout the pothole marshes and glacial lakes. We see a young landscape with dry,

knobby mounds and shallow, wet bowls – the "tracks" of glaciers that melted just 13,000 to 12,000 years ago. Valuable deposits of gravel and sand lie where they were strewn by the glaciers or meltwater streams. Those pulses of water from the decaying ice also formed wide valleys that now carry much smaller rivers.

But the glaciers left much of north-central Iowa's land tabletop flat, without a distinct natural drainage pattern. To make the fields dry enough for farming, people stepped in to help hurry the water away through drainage ditches and

45

Kay Irelan

Ron Johnson

Lowell Washburn

The depths of Iowa's land contain geologic materials that provide vital groundwater resources to wells for drinking water. Also, landfills are excavated into the earth to bury the leftovers of our daily lives. Plastic drainage tile is laid beneath the ground to hurry infiltrating water away from poorly drained fields. It is important to understand the diversity of geologic deposits across the state and how suitable they are for different purposes.

through clay and plastic tile. Indeed, for more than a century, landowners have tiled, ditched, and drained the region to convert its marshes to some of the world's premier farmland. Water now runs off the land through these drainage ways instead of soaking into the sponge-like wetlands.

Alongside, and beneath this northern Iowa pothole country lie landscapes once locked in permafrost. To the east,

in a fifteen-county region centered on Waterloo, weathered boulders still work their way to the surface. These stones, carried from the north during an earlier glaciation more than 500,000 years ago, lie scattered in pastures or piled by farmers in fencerows. Abundant groundwater reaches the surface in springs and rivers and in peaty wetlands, called fens, which also support rare plant and animal communities.

In the northwest portions of Iowa, most evidence of the tundra and glaciers has been covered by layers of windblown loess and modified by erosion from a network of streams. Broad valleys and open uplands roll to the horizon, reminiscent of the ranch country of the Dakotas. But time and weather have exposed tips of the state's oldest bedrock, the Sioux Quartzite, which pokes to the surface in northwest Lyon County. The ancient reddish rock formed from sediments in coastal waters more than 1.6 billion years ago. The famous Pipestone quarries

Right: Non-renewable sand and gravel resources are contained beneath Iowa's land. (Worth County) The location of economic mineral and stone materials needs to be part of long-range planning. Far right: The rivers that thread Iowa's land are important avenues of commerce as well as valuable wildlife habitat. (Mississippi River, Jackson County)

Tim Kemmis

Clay Smith

in southwestern Minnesota are in this same distinct red rock formation, which is regarded as sacred ground by Native American tribes. Ironically, the state's youngest bedrock – sandstone, shale, chalk, and limestone less than 100 million years old – lies directly against the oldest. These "newer" sediments formed in shallow seas confined by cliffs of the old Sioux Quartzite.

While it may challenge our senses to imagine such geologic forces at work over eons, Iowans can watch some

landscape changes happening every day. For example, up to 10 percent of the state's surface is in floodplains, where flowing water carves valleys and deposits sediment along ever-changing river corridors. The Flood of 1993 dramatically showed many Iowans the geologic power of moving water.

We also can try to visualize past events that have shaped Iowa streams. The relatively wide valleys of the Des Moines, Skunk, and other rivers suggest the huge volumes of water that scoured their channels as the ice sheets melted. Some people

RHYTHMS OF LIFE

Essay and photo by Lowell Washburn

At first glance, the winter marsh appears as void and uninhabited as the dark side of the moon. The temperature hovers near zero, and at this season there is no din of bird song to greet the rising sun. As you stroll across the silent expanse of this frozen world, you suddenly get the feeling that this particular piece of real estate is no less remote than a Canadian wilderness.

But first impressions can be deceiving. A closer inspection reveals that the marsh is criss-crossed by a myriad of bird and mammal tracks. These tracks are the winter chronicles of the furred and feathered denizens that call this place home. It is here, in the stark freshness of last night's snowfall, that a human explorer can find nature's version of the daily newspaper. Like most good papers, the snow features information on social gatherings, social strife, and tragedy. It tells where the pheasants are roosting, which weed seed buffets are currently most popular with local rodent populations, and where a resident weasel has set up headquarters beneath a forgotten rock pile.

But for those who desire to go beyond the light reading, animal tracks can also provide a glimpse into a world that urbanized humans have largely forgotten. It is the harsh reality of predator and prey, a realm where the world is neatly divided into two categories. One is the hunter, the other the hunted. In this high-stakes game of survival there are no politics, no trade-offs, no compromise. There is simply a winner and a loser.

The tense balance between predator and prey is amazingly delicate. And in spite of intense human pressures on the environment, the fragile rhythm somehow endures. The basic premise is simple. Prey species, such as mice and rabbits, have a stunning capacity for reproduction. Predators, like the fox or hawk, do not.

Follow the tracks and you'll see how the system works. Here, in the fresh snow, are the briefly recorded episodes of close encounters, hard chases, and near misses. Sometimes there is a widening pink spot in the snow where one life has ended so that another might continue. This uneasy relationship – this struggle for survival – becomes the very essence of the rhythm of life.

The latest set of tracks offers a good example of the rhythm in action. Near the edge of the cattails, a hungry rabbit has ventured into the open to girdle bark from a clump of sumacs. This obviously foolish move does not go unnoticed by the adult redtail perched in a nearby oak. The hawk, also hungry, bobs its head and launches the attack. Sensing its mistake, the winter-lean rabbit flees for cover. Although the escaping animal is soon covering ground with impressive two-foot leaps, the hawk is already halfway across the marsh. As the redtail closes, the cottontail begins a series of evasive maneuvers that buy a few more seconds of life. The raptor mimics the moves and at last the forms converge.

A rabbit dies. A hawk feeds. The natural rhythm continues.

have witnessed the formation of oxbows and backwaters following floods. The wind still sculpts active sand dunes in a few places along the Mississippi, Upper Iowa, Des Moines, and Cedar rivers.

People tend to think of the landscape as permanent and stable. But Iowa's floodplains, hillsides, gullies, and even fractured bedrock are dynamic and changing. Sometimes people have become a major force in those changes. We now have the technology, the equipment, and the power to shape our environment – sometimes subtly, sometimes dramatically, sometimes purposefully, sometimes unintentionally. We have become geologic forces, as anyone knows who has watched a dam being built or seen a road construction crew at work.

Just look around Iowa. It is one of the most intensively used and frequently disturbed landscapes in the country. Even farmers, who turn over only the upper few inches of most of our landscape every year, have assumed earth-moving powers. Thus, while we live on an earth fashioned by nature and time, we've often used our machines, and our whims, to alter the environment around us.

The landscape is where all human activity takes place, and learning to live with it is essential. If we understand its building blocks, however – the bedrock, the soil, the water, the air, and their inherent relationships – then we can protect the land and its heritage, our heritage.

Land is the foundation for our cities and towns, and for all other forms of life. (Des Moines skyline)

Soil: A Fertile Filter

Shooting star

Jack-in-the-pulpit

Luna moth

On a warm May day, when the wild plums are blooming and the oak leaves have begun to unfurl, plunge your fingers into the rich soil of an about-to-be-planted corn field. Or crumble the tiny clods as you poke the last potatoes into the garden plot. Or brush aside the moldering leaves as you pluck a fresh morel at the edge of the woodlot. Then breathe, deeply.

Farmers, gardeners, foresters, and mushroom hunters love the aroma of moist, fertile soil. Children instinctively run their fingers through it; they may squeal with delight as they feel, throw, explore, and taste the very ground they're sitting upon. Just as infants snuggle for comfort in their mothers' arms, we all feel drawn to the earth's soft, living, fragrant skin.

In Iowa, we see that connection clearly, daily. More than half of our state is prime farmland – the rich, black soil that has become the standard for agriculture. Iowa's special land can grow some of the best crops in the world. Our economy, literally and figuratively, is rooted in the soil. Many of us can trace our heritage to the farm families who have worked that precious soil for generations. Even though we have manipu-

lated the soil to fit our human wants and needs by replacing diverse prairies, wetlands, and forests with orderly fields and straight roads, it's still the basis for our livelihoods.

We may grieve, therefore, when we see that soil mis-treated. Our stomachs may tighten when we see a bulldozed construction site, the raw scar of a gouged stream bank, layers of windblown topsoil in the winter snowdrifts, or gullies carved between the corn rows by a heavy rain.

By the same token, we value healthy soil and land. Farmers are understandably proud when neighbors admire their thriving cropfields. Naturalists praise the diversity of a prairie remnant, the majesty of a mature forest, or the richness of life in a wetland. City dwellers may long to walk in a park, sit in the shade of an oak, or splash in a stream that is the lifeblood of our land. At every meal, we nourish our bodies with the bounty of our soil. Thus, in so many ways, the quality of our lives really depends upon the quality of our soil.

Still, sometimes, we take soil and its services for granted. We may not fully appreciate this thin veneer of land – just the

Iowa's agricultural heritage is rooted in generations of farm families working the land and its soil. This Amish woman and boy harvest a grain crop near Kalona in Washington County.

John M. Zielinski

upper few feet – that allows life to exist on Earth. Perhaps we don't realize that nature's forces have manufactured that soil from "parent" earth materials. Soils form slowly, in response to the weather, the lay of the land, and the presence of living and decaying organisms. We struggle to comprehend the 200 to 1,000 years that it took the water, wind, ice, animals, and plants to transform those raw materials into just one inch of topsoil.

We may forget that the soil that enables us to sustain life is itself an extraordinary living community. A spoonful of soil may contain more than 6 billion micro-organisms, a number equal to the human population of the Earth. The earthworms in a single acre of soil can move and aerate 100 tons of soil annually. They may dig 800,000 tunnels, which carry rainwater into and through the soil. Snakes, turtles, insects, and small mammals also burrow into the soil, cultivating it from below.

Brian Button

Photographic Services, University of Iowa

Ron Johnson

Stan Mitchem

Soil loosened for cultivation can be lost to wind erosion (upper left), water erosion (middle), or gully erosion (above and right), and can enable the escape of unused agricultural chemicals into the water and air (lower left).

Larger animals walk on it, dig in it, and rely on its plant products to survive.

Truly, that soil community embraces and physically supports everything that lives on our land. Plants not only sink their roots into the soil, they also draw nutrients from it. Fertile, stable, well-managed soil nurtures a rich plant community that in turn feeds abundant animal life. Those plants also produce life-giving oxygen and use carbon dioxide from the air to produce more green matter. Locked up in that vegetation, then stored as humus in the soil, the carbon is not released into the atmosphere, but is sequestered. This reduces the greenhouse effect and the potential problems of climate change.

The soil's intricate matrix of roots and decaying vegetation and minerals and micro-organisms acts like a sponge to soak up rainwater and snowmelt. This living sponge also can cleanse, recirculate, renew, filter, and store that water, then gently release it again to plant cells or into clear streams. The remarkable soil community, this natural purification system,

UNCLE MERRIS ON THE STRUCTURE OF THE SOIL

Essay by Michael Carey

Natural Resources Conservation Service

Yesterday a fog rolled in and a soft drizzle turned into rain some fifty miles from here. So today, in response, the creeks have risen. And in the middle of the soggy bottom a huge, wet, silver snake begins to shimmer and shine. "The river remembers its bed," Uncle Merris always told me. "The Corps of Engineers can straighten all the banks they want, but the river remembers. Ask any farmer and he'll tell you."

I had gotten stuck, almost buried, in gumbo one too many times to doubt him – the black glue sticking to the axles and wheels on my tractor and disc and then hardening. "It's worse than cement," he'd remind me, "keep it off of your equipment. Wash everything as soon as you muddy it or you may never be able to get it clean." He knew the power in the thing he was tending. What dark forces lay hidden in the memory of the soil. He worked it all his life, but he feared it too and respected it. "Wasn't the dark life of the rich soil, the richest in the world, death really and beautiful decay? Hadn't billions upon billions of living things laid down their short lives for us to stand on and in and to plow? Isn't that what we mean by *organic* matter? Wasn't every farmer in the whole world trying to make money, in the end, from the lives and sacrifice of others? Wasn't everything in this fertile land floating on a sea of death? If for one second we realized how many lives were sacrificed to help us, now, make a living, we would tend the grave more carefully. We wouldn't let one sacred ounce of it slip away down the Missouri or give it away, as so many have before us, to the distant swamps of the Mississippi Delta."

"One half of prairie earth," he said "is air. One half of the earth we stand on is sky. Heaven has come and made the ground fragile. Ask the wind and the water and the worms. Ask all the microorganisms that breed and seed and feed on what feeds you. Step knowingly!"

Once again the white corn and ripening beans bend themselves when they hear the distant roar roaring closer. In these painfully changing times, there is nothing stopping whatever happens. Whatever happened yesterday fifty miles north and east of here matters desperately today to me *and* to you, to people who may have never left home, or looked up and wondered what it is that is coming, who put this food in our hands, what in God's name they were doing on this earth so long.

Bruce A. Morrison

Cultivated rows of soybeans use soils developed where native grasslands once thrived. Intensive cultivation gives Iowa's land the appearance of a well-tended garden.

also neutralizes our wastes, breaking down toxins into harmless substances. And when plants or animals die, the soil recycles them into new soil, to grow new plants that feed new animals.

Soils often are complex and unique. In fact, scientists have identified at least 11,000 different soils in Iowa. These soils vary in how they were formed, their physical structure, their landscape position, their ability to hold water, the plants and animals they support, how easily they erode, and their chemical compositions. Each soil behaves and looks differently, has distinct capabilities and limitations, and ultimately is influenced by a host of factors acting upon it.

Some soils work hard to help manufacture food and fiber used by people. A few soils cling precariously to steep, rocky slopes, yet they still yield scenic beauty and wildlife habitat. Other soils have left the state, swept away by the winds and waters of change. Like people, soils that lose their health may no longer contribute to the community, but with proper care, they can remain vigorous and productive.

But the soil community has been slipping away. In the 150 years since we began intensely clearing, plowing, and cultivating the land that once supported our prairies and forests and wetlands, the steeper croplands have lost about half of their original topsoil. Erosion has stripped off the rich surface layer, including organic matter, nutrients, and living organisms. The displaced soil becomes just sediment – dumped into streams and swept into ditches or the atmosphere. That soil had been forming for thousands of years, yet in just a century and a half, we've depleted 50 percent of that original precious resource on our hilly lands.

We've also stamped the soil, and the landscape, with the imprints of our human activities. People build roads and like straight lines. In place of a mosaic of diverse vegetation,

Natural Resources Conservation Service

Gene Alexander

Lowell Washburn

controlled by nature's flowing contours, we've girdled the land with a geometric pattern of highways, fields, fences, and utility lines. Instead of leaving the soil anchored in permanent plant cover, we now till and plant the fields, harvest the crops, then often leave the earth exposed to the elements for half the year.

Even the soil that stays in place can lose its quality. Nutrients may leach out, or salts can accumulate. Chemicals can kill soil microbes and interfere with biological activity. Heavy equipment or livestock can pack down soil layers and hamper water infiltration. Thus, runoff and flooding increase, leaving less water available for plant growth. Erosion and

Iowa's annual corn harvest and checkbook balance reflect the ingenuity of farmers, the judicious application of farm chemicals, government farm policies, environmental regulations, profitable conservation measures, and the strength of a partnership with land, soil, and water resources.

Lynn Betts

When the land does well for its owner and the owner does well by his land – when both end up better by reason of their partnership – then we have conservation. When one or the other grows poorer, either in substance, or in character, or in responsiveness to sun, wind, and rain, then we have something else, and it is something we do not like.
– Aldo Leopold, The Farmer as a Conservationist, 1939 speech

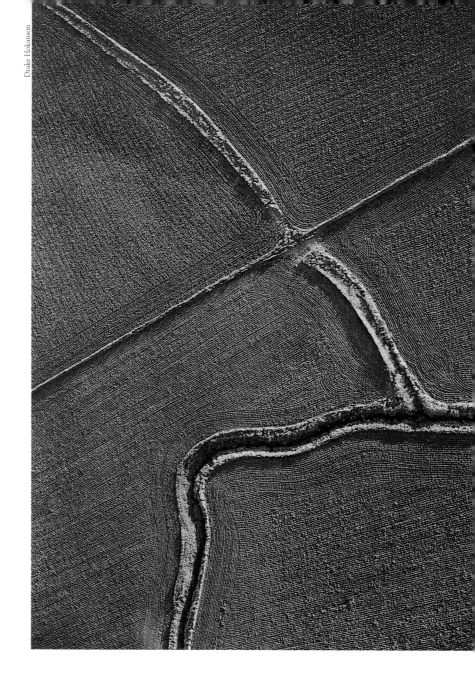

Drake Hokanson

Aerial view of cropland interrupted by a stream, a drainage ditch, and a fence line. Iowa's land is working land. Most of it is used, not idle, and is focused on the job of nurturing cultivated plants from extraordinarily productive soils.

intensive cropping can destroy organic matter and diminish a soil's vitality, productivity, and water-holding capacity.

And when the soil suffers, the land suffers. Indeed, we all suffer. Crop yields fall. Sediment clogs road ditches and culverts, carries contaminants, pollutes drinking water supplies, damages fish and wildlife habitat, and degrades recreational lakes and streams.

Fortunately, many good stewards treasure every particle of our soil. They guard its health, appreciate its crops, respect its integrity, and protect it from abuse and neglect. They know that healthy soil – whether it grows corn, oaks, bluestem, or cattails – is the foundation of our very existence.

Blue flag iris

Bottle gentian

Tree frog

Water: A Life-Giving Cycle

Whether it comes from a sprinkle, a downpour, or a blizzard – a river, a lake, or an underground aquifer – water gives us life.

We might think first of water as an essential liquid that we must drink. Without it, we die. It's a critical, yet sometimes inconspicuous, part of our air, our land, our bodies. Likewise, our crops must have water to grow. And water drives the weather cycles: the winds, the rains, the storms, the clouds, the ever-changing warmth and cold that affect nearly everything we do.

This amazing little molecule, just one oxygen atom bonded with two hydrogen atoms, is priceless yet free. It falls from the sky for anyone to capture and use. Iowa annually receives about thirty-two inches of precipitation, enough to average two and one-half feet of water spread over the entire state, or enough to provide about 11 million gallons per person.

But where does all that water go? About two inches of our moisture evaporates from trees and plants before it can even reach the earth; it returns almost immediately to the atmosphere. Surprisingly little water, only about four inches of our total rain and snowfall, runs directly into our rivers and lakes. Another two inches soak into the groundwater system. The vast majority, about twenty-four inches or three-fourths of the water that falls, lingers temporarily in the soil where it sustains our bountiful crops and lush, green vegetation. Like living pumps, the plants draw the moisture from the soil, pull it through the roots, stems, and leaves, and process it into growing cells. That liberal water supply, along with our temperate climate, rich soil, and favorable slope of land, makes Iowa one of the most productive places on Earth.

To maintain the cycle, our land and atmosphere constantly recirculate and reuse that water. It rises into the air, through a thunderstorm, and back to earth. It is stored in shallow lakes and rivers and deep rock aquifers, soaked up by plants, gulped down by animals, season after season. We humans may interrupt the process as we borrow water for our own uses: drinking, sewage treatment, industry, recreation, and irrigation. But eventually the water cycle continues.

Our water resources also shape and beautify our landscape. Two of the nation's mightiest rivers, the Mississippi and Missouri, embrace Iowa's land. The giant watercourses run nearly 500 miles along our borders, covering more than

200,000 acres. Their history – of geologic spectacles, Indian cultures, early explorers, abundant wildlife, and industrial development – mirrors Iowa history. We revere those waters and the scenic valleys where they flow. But we also ask much of these places, for they sustain cities and industries; provide biological habitats; attract suburban developers; host greenbelt recreationists; yield sand, gravel, rock, and groundwater resources; and provide space for overflowing rivers.

We recognize, too, the way we've rebuilt those rivers for our own purposes. On the Mississippi, locks and dams, frequent dredging, and diversion dikes now maintain a passage deep enough for barge traffic. We have built a series of artificial pools joined by regulated channels, replacing the maze of wild chutes and sloughs that once wandered across the valley between the bluffs. Still, the Mississippi Valley remains rich in fish and waterfowl resources. Tourists seek its scenery and history. Boaters explore its islands and backwaters.

On the Missouri, however, engineers saved less of the original river. They built huge reservoirs to capture upstream snowmelt and straightened the meandering channel into a rock-lined canal. Now the Missouri, which once swelled across the bottomlands in the spring and slithered among sandbars in the summer, marches uniformly past our western border. Its water level rises and falls not so much with the upstream precipitation as with the computer-operated gates of dams in the Dakotas and Montana.

Between these two giants on Iowa's east and west coasts

Roger Hill

WATERFORMS
Essay by Jean Cutler Prior

With the melting of snow and the puddling of raindrops, water gathers for its innumerable journeys throughout Iowa. As it flows along, water may become part of a kettlehole, a marsh, a farm pond, a river, a flood, an aquifer, a fen, a cave, a spring, or a waterfall. In all of its aspects, water adds fluid beauty to the landscape. Both above and below ground, water is an ever-present geologic force as well as a vital natural resource.

Thousands of years ago, water in the form of glaciers carried the raw materials of much of Iowa's present landscape into the state. In turn, the melting of glaciers laid the courses of most rivers seen on today's maps. Even the state's bedrock foundation, those picturesque ledges and bluffs along some of Iowa's river valleys, originated as layers of sediment settling on ancient sea floors, along coastlines, and in stream channels millions of years ago.

Iowa's geological past supplied the basic earth materials that contain our present surface and groundwater resources. These materials not only shape the form that water takes on the land, they also determine how fast and how far water moves underground, and where it can be tapped for wells. Geologic deposits affect groundwater's natural quality as well as its vulnerability to contamination from the land surface.

Photos by Photographic Services, University of Iowa

Michael Bounk

Above left: Water takes many forms, such as gathering storm clouds, rising water vapor, and dripping cave stalactites. Left: The chemical composition of cave formations provides clues to past climatic conditions in Iowa. Above right: Amish men cut blocks of ice from a farm pond near Kalona, in Washington County.

flows an incredible network of tributaries – more than 70,000 miles of tiny creeks, winding streams, and robust rivers. These valleys served as pathways for Indian travelers and fur trappers and European settlers. Railroads, highways, recreational trails, and greenbelts still follow the corridors. Cities have grown from the villages that first sprouted along the riverbanks. Through the decades, Iowans have plied the inland rivers in steamboats and harnessed their waters for power. Enterprising pioneers built more than 1,000 water-driven mills to grind wheat and

saw lumber. We've dipped our drinking water from these streams, dumped our wastes into them, and fought their floods. We've straightened, dammed, canoed, and fished them. We've also built more than 25,000 bridges across them.

The water that feeds our streams also fills our lakes. In some of the forty-eight remaining glacial lakes, water lilies bloom in the shallows. Beds of aquatic plants often grow from the clear depths. Walleyes and perch sometimes prowl the gravel bars. Glacial boulders may ring the shorelines. More than 32,000 acres of water trace their origin to ice sheets that gouged these lake basins more than 12,000 years ago.

Not satisfied with the natural lakes, people have im-pounded another 148,000 acres of water to fill large reservoirs

Paul VanDorpe

Photographic Services, University of Iowa

Lowell Washburn

Right: Drinking water from underground aquifers is used by 78 percent of Iowans. Middle: Water sometimes cycles from the atmosphere back to Earth with a dramatic counterpoint. Far right: In its continuing cycle, water stops temporarily to encase a bittersweet vine in ice.

and artificial lakes built for recreation. These structures may have earthen dams, rip-rapped shorelines, and mud bottoms, but we're still fascinated by bodies of water. We love to swim and fish in them, to sail and ski upon them, and to build our houses beside them.

Everybody likes lakes, it seems, but wetlands are another matter. Shallow marshes once teemed with birds, animals, and plant life, however their rich basins also became some of the richest cropland on Earth. And now, virtually all of the countless tiny ponds and potholes that once dotted Iowa have been drained and farmed. We've slowly come to recognize the value of wetlands, however. Marshes can slow floods, store water, provide wildlife habitat, neutralize pollutants, digest wastes, and trap sediment. To reap those benefits, government agencies and private landowners have built nearly 30,000 acres of artificial or restored marshes in recent years, doubling the acreage of remaining natural wetlands.

These aquatic ecosystems have an abundant array of plant and animal life. Algae drift in the water or cling to the rocks and submerged logs. Rooted plants sway in the current, reaching for the sunlight. Snails and caddisflies forage in the gravel. One-celled protozoans become food for water fleas, which in turn are eaten by dragonfly larvae, which are food for fish, which can be eaten by herons or by people.

Still, beneath all the marshes and land and lakes and rivers, seeping through gravel and rock, flows yet more water – Iowa's groundwater. It's mostly hidden from view, but groundwater from wells supplies the drinking water for 78 percent of

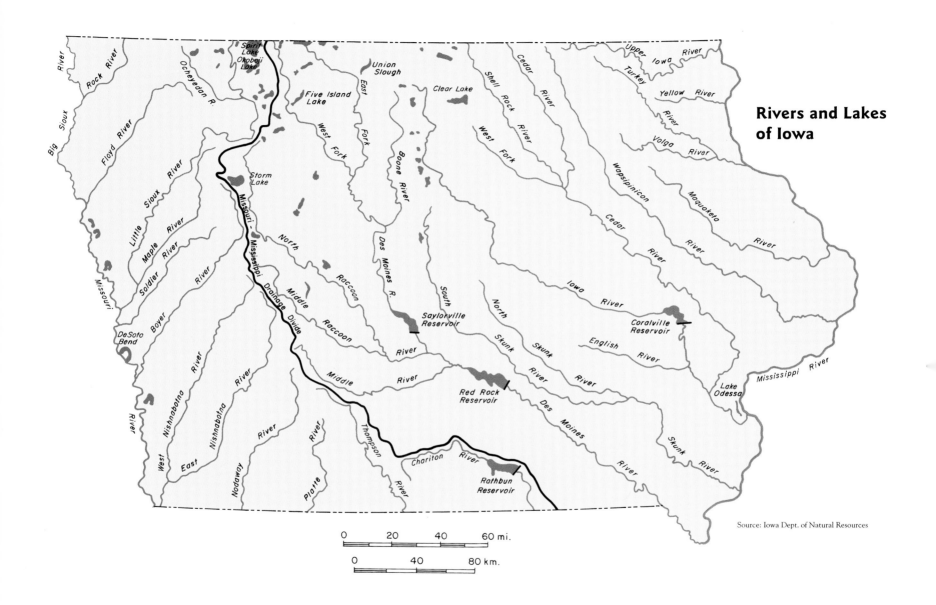

Rivers and Lakes of Iowa

Source: Iowa Dept. of Natural Resources

Big Sioux River

Rock River

Ocheyedan R.

Spirit Lake
Okoboji Lake

Five Island Lake

Union Slough

Clear Lake

Upper Iowa River

Turkey River

Yellow River

Volga River

Floyd River

East Fork

West Fork

Shell Rock River

Cedar River

Little Sioux River

Maple River

Soldier River

Storm Lake

West Fork

Wapsipinicon River

Maquoketa River

Missouri River

Missouri Mississippi Drainage Divide

North Raccoon River

Boone River

Des Moines R.

Cedar River

River

Boyer River

Middle Raccoon River

South

Saylorville Reservoir

Iowa River

Coralville Reservoir

DeSoto Bend

West Nishnabotna River

East Nishnabotna River

River

Middle River

North Skunk River

Skunk River

English River

River

Red Rock Reservoir

Lake Odessa

Mississippi River

Nodaway River

Platte River

Thompson River

Chariton River

Rathbun Reservoir

Des Moines River

Skunk River

0   20   40   60 mi.

0   40   80 km.

62

Iowans. The rest drink surface water from lakes and streams. Groundwater occasionally bubbles up at springs or flows from artesian wells, such as the public well in Benson Park just west of Clarion. We drill wells to tap groundwater, and surface waters ever-so-slowly recharge it. Although often buried far underground, it's still vulnerable to pollution and much harder to clean up than water exposed to air and sunshine.

Focused as we are on the quantity of our water resources, Iowans must protect the quality as well. Before we began to exploit our landscape by plowing prairies, draining wetlands, grubbing out forests, straightening rivers, and developing lakeshores, our waters usually ran clear. Fish, mussels, aquatic birds, water-loving animals, and plant life thrived. Underground aquifers stored pristine water, and springs gushed with pure flows that had been filtered through layers of soil and rock.

But the purity of the water can be only as good as the integrity of the watershed, the land from which it flows. As we've changed the surface of the land, is it any wonder that people have muddied those waters? Where rainfall used to slowly ooze into marshes or trickle through prairie vegetation, the water now falls on crop ground across two-thirds of the state. Too often, the runoff rushes into rivers and streams, carrying with it topsoil and agricultural chemicals. Silt chokes fish and other aquatic life, clouds the water, and reduces the sunlight that reaches algae and submerged plants.

Iowa farmers annually apply more than 3 billion pounds

WHAT'S YOUR WATERSHED ADDRESS?

Essay by
Larry A. Stone

Dark Sky – Canvasbacks © Maynard Reece

Where do you live?

Besides having a street or county road address, we each live in a very distinct watershed. The land, like the back of a duck, sheds water. Rainwater and melting snow from the land around us run downhill. The water follows a specific path, flowing into a series of lakes, wetlands, and streams, in an ever-expanding link – ultimately to the sea.

Thus, the quality of our watershed determines the quality of our water. Larger watersheds will move more water. Certain soils filter water more completely, or erode more easily, than others. Steep slopes or paved parking lots speed runoff. Wetlands, forests, and farmland conservation retard the flow and reduce flooding.

We need to ask questions about the land that funnels our water to us. On its way, does our water flow through a park or a feedlot or a prairie or a housing development? How carefully do upstream neighbors dispose of their sewage, use pesticides, or recycle toxic wastes?

What about the water that leaves our property? Do we consider downstream friends when we maintain sewers or septic tanks, plant crops, fertilize lawns, dump garbage, wash cars, or discard household chemicals?

Clean water starts with the small decisions we make in our own communities – in our watersheds.

Gary Hightshoe, Iowa State University

Roger Hill

Lynn Betts

Clay Smith

Water is stored on the landscape in natural lakes, such as the rounded shores of Big Spirit, Marble, and Hottes, in Dickinson County (above) and by constructed embankments that form farm ponds (near right).

Above: Natural meanders and oxbow lakes form riparian wetland habitat along the East Fork Des Moines River, in Kossuth County. These waters contrast sharply with the confined flow and straightened channel of the Little Sioux River in Monona County (right).

of chemical fertilizers and 45 million pounds of pesticides to their corn and soybean fields. Should we be surprised, then, to learn that agricultural pesticides can be detected in nearly every sample of rainfall taken during the growing season and that the chemicals show up in 26 percent of groundwater samples and 78 percent of surface waters sampled? Scientists may differ on the impacts of agricultural chemicals on human health or the environment, but few dispute their wide dispersal.

Nitrogen from farm and lawn fertilizers, livestock ma-

nure, and municipal and industrial wastes also enter our land and rivers and eventually travel down the Mississippi River system. The accumulated discharges of these pollutants into the Gulf of Mexico have reduced the amount of oxygen there, causing the hypoxic zone, an area in the Gulf with very little aquatic life. Researchers have calculated that Iowa may contribute nearly 25 percent of the nitrates that the Mississippi delivers to the Gulf. Studies continue on the exact sources of the excess nitrogen, the long-term impacts, and strategies to reduce the nitrogen problem.

Fortunately, our land has a tremendous capacity to filter out, neutralize, and recycle sediment and other effluents before they reach the water. Our water ecosystems also can purify many pollutants, but we must not overload these natural sanitation systems. For example, livestock manure can fertilize and enrich our farms. If the waste is spread too heavily on the land, however, or if it does not have time to decompose before rains wash it downstream, it can poison our streams. Discharges from factories, municipal sewage and private septic systems also may enter rivers, either intentionally or by accident.

Many Iowa streams and lakes fail to meet federal clean water standards. Problems range from silt to fertilizer to agricultural chemicals to industrial wastes to algae to sewage to livestock manure. We can't expect our waters to return to prehistoric purity, but how dirty is too dirty? In an agricultural state, how much can we minimize siltation? Should we tolerate some level of pollution from farm chemicals or manure? Shouldn't we be equally concerned about lawn chemicals and oil from vehicles that run off city streets, parking lots, or suburban lawns? Can our industries use our water, then return it to a river even cleaner than they found it? What if pollutants enter our groundwater supplies? How can we clean up those vital, vulnerable aquifers? And will we have enough pure water in the future? Can we use and reuse our precious water, then leave it clean and plentiful enough for others to use?

As we ponder these questions, we also should consider this reality – water, clean water, truly is our lifeblood.

Lynn Betts

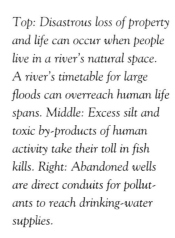

Ron Johnson

John Walkowiak

Lowell Washburn

Top: Disastrous loss of property and life can occur when people live in a river's natural space. A river's timetable for large floods can overreach human life spans. Middle: Excess silt and toxic by-products of human activity take their toll in fish kills. Right: Abandoned wells are direct conduits for pollutants to reach drinking-water supplies.

65

Indigo bunting

Iowa Resources Today: Status and Trends

Purple coneflower

Striped skunk

With the benefit of 150 years of hindsight, we could bemoan the sometimes-flawed mural Iowans have painted on the land as we developed our state and used our resources. The push to build productive farms, cities, and industries probably overshadowed a concern for natural areas. People may have taken the forests, marshes, and prairies for granted and assumed rivers always would run clean. Who could imagine that abundant wildlife might disappear? The industrious people were too busy to notice the abuse of their natural resources or the scope of their loss.

But there's hope. We're developing a new ethic, a fresh outlook, with pride in our land stewardship. Iowans want to live in a sustainable society. We're joining citizen groups that work effectively for conservation. We believe we can improve the quality of life in Iowa's future.

To meet that goal, we must assess the health of our land and realize that the diagnosis reflects our own attitudes and actions. We can be proud of our progress, but we must admit where we've fallen short. As we look ahead, we're thinking of our children and grandchildren and the community they'll have to build upon. Perhaps we need to repair parts of that foundation, to repaint some tarnished images, and to consider the well-being of all the citizens of that land community.

As we catalog our resources, most of us would begin with water. We drink it, swim in it, and catch fish from it. We can't live without it. Yet we're not always sure that it is really safe or clean.

We can boast that about 98 percent of the state's 1,128 community water systems meet federal standards, but we're not so proud of the 55 percent of private wells that are tainted with coliform bacteria, pesticides, or excessive nitrates.

Our lakes and streams, while not pristine, may be cleaner than in the early 1900s, when they were fouled with sewage and industrial wastes. But federal studies of our surface waters still note contamination ranging from fertilizer to agricultural chemicals to industrial wastes to sewage to livestock manure.

Channelization and drainage have damaged many lakes and rivers, but some of our past mistakes can be repaired. We've discovered new remedies, including wetland restorations along the Missouri River and the Iowa River, and more than 170,000 acres of native grasses and trees growing in buffer strips along streams all over the state.

We should do more. We must spend more time and money to monitor livestock wastes, urban runoff, pesticides, sewage facilities, and nonpoint pollution. We can protect rivers and lakes by safeguarding their watersheds, restoring wetlands, and stopping channelization. We can close agricultural drainage wells and control industrial discharges to protect our precious and vulnerable groundwater. Perhaps most of all, we can think about our water whenever we work in a factory, spray a dandelion, spread manure, or flush. And we can consider water as we're working the soil.

Indeed, the quality of our water can be only as good as the quality of the soil that filters it. The topsoil that once grew our prairies, forests, and wetlands – and purified our water – has been eroding away since we removed most of the original plant cover. After only 150 years of statehood, most of our sloping cropland has lost half of its topsoil. Our very heritage has washed into streams, blown across fields and ditches, choked aquatic systems, and transported pesticides and fertilizers.

With 70 percent of the state in cropland that is tilled or

PRICELESS
Essay by Donald R. Farrar

What does it mean, this term "priceless"? Doesn't everything have a price? Is there really anything that enough money can't buy? Not much, but let's list some possibilities. A breath of fresh, clean, clear outdoor air. That can't be purchased in New York or Los Angeles, and often not even in the High Sierras when the coast cities' emissions drift eastward. How about clean, cold water to canoe in, or to fish, or just to splash in on a hot summer afternoon; or the beauty of a million wildflowers sprinkled over a forest floor in the light green shade of early spring; or the comfort of an old tree watching its furry, feathery, and leafy neighbors going about their forest business. Can these be purchased, once they are gone? I think not. These are treasures, still to be found in Iowa, that are truly priceless.

Above, left: Sweet William is a spring woodland wildflower. Middle: A limestone outcrop, flowing creek, and woodland community form a visual oasis in Story County. Below: A painted turtle climbs a log in a cluster of purple prairie clover near a wetland in Story County.

Creek and turtle photos by Roger Hill,
flower photo by John Pearson

Photographic Services, University of Iowa

Corn stubble left on fields during the winter holds soil and moisture in place, helps prevent wind erosion, benefits wintering wildlife, and adds nutrient material to the soil in spring.

Bruce Ehresman

Above: Wood of the white oak is a valuable timber crop, and its colorful foliage is a highlight of the fall season. Right: Increased efforts are underway to monitor the quality of Iowa's surface and groundwaters. (Sny Magill Creek, Clayton County)

Tim McCabe

planted every year, it's no wonder that Iowa is losing its topsoil. We've gotten better, but in 1997, Iowa farms lost more than five tons of soil per acre to wind and water erosion. The losses decreased from ten tons per acre in 1982, but we still lose almost a bushel of soil for every bushel of corn that we grow. It's only a layer less than 1/32 of an inch thick, but it amounts to hauling away and dumping a truckload of soil for each truck-load of grain harvested.

As we try to conserve our soil, we should guard its quality as well. To grow crops, support plants and animals, and process water and air, our soil must be a dynamic resource, filled with essential living organisms. We can protect its health from the ailments of erosion, chemical overuse, weed infestations, and loss of organic matter. Like our own skin, our topsoil is a fragile layer that defends the integrity of a complex, living organism. Future generations depend upon its welfare.

Not only does that soil provide our food, it also grows plants that cleanse and produce our air. Iowans take pride in our fresh air. Because we assume that the air we breathe is clean, we don't often test it.

When we do test our air, we may not like the results. Several Iowa sites have violated air health standards. Each fall, leaf smoke engulfs some towns. Even when it's clear, we can see only 15 to 30 miles, compared with 45 to 90 miles in the early

1800s. Many air-quality problems stem from wasteful use of energy. Burning fossil fuels annually produces about 100 million tons of carbon dioxide in Iowa. Vehicles foul our air with nitrous oxides, toxins, carbon monoxide, waste oil, and palls of smog.

Large-scale livestock operations can generate large-scale manure stenches. Industrial odors taint some communities. But Iowa does not regulate odor-causing chemicals. Nor do we adequately test for toxins in the air, although other studies suggest these pollutants are of concern. Airborne toxins can cause cancer, contaminate our water, or spread across the land.

We have made progress in recent years, however. Gasoline engines burn cleaner, and smokestacks give off fewer emissions. Iowa's air quality may be better than in some other parts of the nation. Still, the problems we do have are magnified by their impacts on older people. Iowa has the nation's highest percentage of residents over age eighty, and we rank fourth in people over sixty-five. Clean air is vital for all of us.

Of course, people aren't the only ones who use air. It's also essential for our animal and plant communities: crops, gardens, green space, natural areas, and preserves.

Take prairie, for example. Many believed this grassland was too poor to grow trees, too barren for settlers. Surprisingly, this "waste" land became the richest on Earth. Once farmers discovered its fertile soil, the prairie community was doomed. The land that is now Iowa opened for settlement in 1833. By 1910, about 97 percent of the prairie had been converted to

Another era of cartoonists brings environmental issues to public attention in the tradition of "Ding" Darling. (Brian Duffy, Des Moines Register)

agriculture. In seventy-seven years – one lifetime – we obliterated an ecosystem.

Today, Iowans once again are protecting bits of prairie. Biologists at Neal Smith National Wildlife Refuge, near Prairie City, are reconstructing 6,000 acres of prairie, complete with elk and bison herds. The Iowa Department of Transportation and many Iowa counties are seeding prairie species in road

McFarland Lake was formed by impounding the waters of a small tributary to the South Skunk River. The site is headquarters for the Story County Conservation Board. County conservation boards play a valuable role in managing and restoring natural areas, as well as offering interpretive opportunities for the public.

rights-of-way. Prairie eventually could cover 600,000 acres along 100,000 miles of roads. Suburbanites tend colorful prairie wildflower gardens. Farmers grow switchgrass to be burned with coal. Cattle raisers use native grass pastures. Prairie plantings

attract a wide variety of birds, small mammals, and butterflies.

But interest in prairies grew slowly. Conservation efforts in the early 1900s by Thomas Macbride and Louis Pammel emphasized woodlands. Finally, in 1946, Iowa State College botanist Ada Hayden published a list of prairie remnants, asking to preserve twenty-two sites with 6,000 acres in ten counties. Many have been destroyed, but state, county, and private groups have protected others. Hayden Prairie State Preserve, 240 acres in Howard County, honors Hayden's work.

Iowa's prairie now covers less than 0.1 percent of the original 28.6 million acres, and half of the remnants may be of poor quality. About 100 preserves protect 5,000 acres of prairie. Private owners control several thousand acres of prairie, with the largest parcels in the Loess Hills and the Little Sioux River valley. Smaller remnants may survive throughout Iowa, but these relics need to be identified and protected from invading trees, overgrazing, and land use changes.

Like prairies, wetlands for decades were considered wasteland that needed to be made "useful." Call them marshes, swamps, or potholes, many have disappeared in the last century – drained or altered for agriculture, industry, cities, and roads.

Iowa has lost 90 percent of its original 4.5 million acres of wetlands, especially in the north-central prairie pothole region, which became world-class cropland. We also dredged and ditched rivers and adjoining sloughs and lowlands. We have laid about 800,000 miles of drainage tile. That's seven times the length of our road system.

This restored wetland is the site of a former sand and gravel operation. Such lowland sites are often water-filled and highly suited for establishing wildlife habitat and recreation areas. (Bob Pyle Marsh, Story County)

The vibrant bloom of native prairie species brightens the view for travelers of Interstate 35 north of Ames. The Iowa Department of Transportation reestablished this roadside prairie.

Photos on pages 70–71 by Roger Hill

But now we realize what we've lost, and Iowans have begun restoring wetlands. Farmers are rebuilding wetlands on about 10,000 acres of land in the federal Conservation Reserve Program. The North American Waterfowl Management Plan and the federal Wetlands Reserve and Emergency Wetlands Reserve Programs also are helping restore wetlands on another 91,000 acres, with more planned.

Although we've made a good start by plugging tiles and pooling water to reconstruct wetlands, we may not be able to duplicate the unique habitats of the original communities.

Prairie potholes formed in level terrain, with little natural drainage. But we typically rebuild wetlands downstream, capturing water from tiles or ditches.

Nevertheless, Iowans have new regard for wetland functions and aesthetics. We see how both natural and reconstructed wetlands filter our water and trap sediment. Wetlands hold floods, then release waters slowly. People seek wetlands'

Bruce Ehresman

Lowell Washburn

People can ensure that other forms of life also thrive on Iowa's land. Reproduction of our native wildlife populations is dependent on protecting their habitat. Above: baby opossums. Left: Raccoon twins in their hollow den tree.

natural beauty to hunt, fish, and watch wildlife. Water in wetlands recharges aquifers. We've accepted the wetland as a respected member of our natural community.

While heavily damaged, Iowa's forests escaped the almost complete devastation we imposed on our other natural systems. They were spared partly because they grow on land unsuited for other crops and partly because people prize trees for wildlife, shade, windbreaks, aesthetics, recreation, and wood products. Trees can boost urban property values as much as 15 percent, and reduce heating and cooling costs nearly 30 percent. Iowa wood industries also support 7,000 jobs, with an annual payroll of $142 million. In northeast Iowa, tourists spend $6 million annually to see fall leaf colors.

Early settlers saw trees as commodities to be used or as impediments to agriculture. Of the 6.7 million acres of forests in Iowa, nearly two-thirds, more than 4 million acres, had been lost to clearing, grazing, logging, or fuelwood cutting by 1900. The destruction continued with intensive crop and livestock farming. By 1974, only 1.5 million acres of woodlands remained in Iowa. Since then, our forests have rebounded to about 2.1 million acres, due to less grazing and to more tree planting. Some cities have even developed forest-like canopies.

But these forests aren't just in public parks. With more than 92 percent of our woodlands in private hands, individual decisions will shape our future forests. People who own woods for hunting or other hobbies may manage the forest very differently than did the farmers who used the timber for grazing

Our good fortune can't possibly last any longer than our natural resources.
– Will Rogers, 1928

Larry Stone

Young pileated woodpeckers look out from their hole in a dead elm tree near the Turkey River.

or firewood cutting. Yes, Iowa is a farm state, but farm fields don't preclude forests. Our people like trees, and we're welcoming their return to our diverse green space.

These samples of our original landscape can and do attract wildlife, but small habitat remnants obviously cannot sustain the array of birds and animals that once lived here. The bison, passenger pigeon, whooping crane, and sturgeon have given way to raccoons, white-tailed deer, red-winged blackbirds, and channel catfish. Today's wildlife live with cropfields, scattered forests, and muddy waters. But even common birds and animals enrich our lives. By U.S. Fish and Wildlife Service estimates, more than one million Iowans watch wildlife, hunt, or go fishing.

Whether we continue to enjoy wildlife depends, of course, on habitat. If wild creatures are adapted to our land uses, they can prosper. Deer have flourished, even with hunters annually taking about 100,000 white-tails. Some cities and parks allow hunting to control deer. Woodchucks and cottontail rabbits invade gardens. Canada geese take over ponds on golf courses and city parks.

Sometimes, wildlife species respond to people's help. We've brought back wild turkeys and river otters by releasing birds and animals from other states. Peregrine falcons, wiped out by the pesticide DDT in the 1960s, are nesting again, aided by captive breeding. Bald eagle numbers have rebounded spectacularly. Trumpeter swans, released in the wild, are breeding once more after a 100-year absence.

Other animal populations have dropped because of human disturbances. The ovenbird, veery, and cerulean warbler declined with the break-up of large forests. Pintails, yellow-

Barn owls hunt southern Iowa grasslands and nest in old trees or barns. (Endangered species)

Bruce Ehresman

headed blackbirds, and rails decreased with their wetlands. As grasslands disappeared, so did short-eared owls and upland sandpipers. About eighty animals, from bobcats to bats and from snails to butterflies, are now threatened or endangered.

Loss of these habitats destroyed plant communities, as well as the wildlife. For example, the endangered western white-fringed prairie orchid and the rare small white lady's slipper were common before their prairie habitat was plowed. Bog willow and brook lobelia inhabited fens (spring-fed bogs), most of which have been destroyed by grazing and draining.

About 150 Iowa plant species have been classified as rare or endangered, while 40 more have not been seen for decades and may no longer grow here. To avoid losing more of these pieces of our heritage, Iowans must protect their habitat.

We also must shield our native species from invaders. House sparrows and European starlings have become pests. Carp have ruined good fishing waters. The zebra mussel, a tiny clam, crowds out native mussels in the Mississippi River and other waters. Leafy spurge and bromegrass invade prairies. Garlic mustard and buckthorn displace other plants in woodlands. Eurasian water milfoil can take over lakes. Purple loosestrife chokes wetlands. With few natural enemies, such exotics disrupt our native communities. Just as we try to keep our own bodies healthy to resist diseases, we must try to keep the land healthy to ward off alien species.

Iowa's archaeological resources, links to our cultural past and environmental history, also are in jeopardy. More than 80

UNCOMMON WILDLIFE IN IOWA

Lowell Washburn

Yellow-headed blackbirds nest over water in the northern Iowa wetlands.

Iowa Dept. of Natural Resources

The blue-spotted salamander likes open, sandy woods and is known to inhabit only two sites in east-central Iowa. (Endangered species)

Ty Smedes

The rare piping plover thrived among once-numerous Missouri River sandbars. (Endangered species)

74

Bobcat sightings are increasing in southern and northeastern Iowa. Their habitat consists of brushy woods, bluffs, and field edges. (Endangered species)

Badgers were once a widespread species on Iowa's open prairie. Today they remain in fragments of limited habitat, digging distinctive oval holes in soft, loose earth materials.

The western worm snake is a secretive creature of the prairie-woodland edge in southern Iowa. (Threatened species)

percent of the state's 19,000 known archaeological sites have been damaged or destroyed by erosion, sand and gravel operations, construction, farming, vandalism, or careless artifact collecting. Many more sites – windows on antiquity – no doubt remain undiscovered. Only 5 percent of the state has been surveyed for these fragile remnants that show the way of life of early Iowans.

Although Iowa laws protect all cemeteries and burials, regardless of age or condition, these and other archaeological sites may be difficult to find and identify. To be able to learn from the 600 generations of native Iowans who were here before Europeans arrived, and to appreciate their culture, we must protect these clues to their legacy.

Healthy land not only works for us, it can be a source of fun and relaxation. People are drawn to the land. It bonds us to ancestors, links us with natural communities, and offers scenery and solitude. Thus, our increasingly urban people long for outdoor recreation. Health-conscious families want trails. Disabled people deserve access. Older citizens have more time to visit parks.

But hikers, campers, canoeists, boaters, snowmobilers, equestrians, bikers, hunters, picnickers, and bird-watchers may compete for the same space. Can we buy sufficient land or develop enough sites to avoid conflict among these groups?

Iowa's innovative County Conservation Board system provides close-to-home recreation. The 99 boards manage nearly 1,500 diverse areas. Private conservation groups also

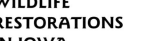

Bald eagle

Trumpeter swan

Wild turkey

American peregrine falcon

Beaver

White-tailed deer (fawn)

Bluebird

Canada goose

Sandhill crane

Prairie chicken

Sharp-tailed grouse

River otter

Eagle and bluebird photos by Ty Smedes; pra
chicken, grouse, and crane photos by Roger
other photos by Lowell Washburn

identify and protect natural areas and wildlife habitat. Our 66 state parks and recreation areas, with more than 53,000 acres, host 10 to 15 million visitors each year. Nearly 2,000 miles of trails traverse those parks and forests.

Add 9,345 acres of state-protected preserves, 40,000 acres of state forests, 318,000 acres of state fish and wildlife areas, and another 190,000 acres of federal lands, yet Iowa still has a smaller proportion of public land than almost any other state. About 600,000 acres of roadside rights-of-way and more than 40,000 acres of railroad corridors could be managed to improve habitat and scenery. But all these lands together cannot meet the demands for recreation. Private landowners can provide some opportunities for hunting, fishing, bird-watching, and enjoyment of the outdoors, but what of the future, with even more pressure on our resources?

Native Iowan Aldo Leopold, writing in *A Sand County Almanac,* understood: "Recreational development is a job not of building roads into lovely country, but of building receptivity into the . . . human mind."

People pressures affect every Iowa resource. For example, Iowa relies on imported fossil fuels – gasoline, natural gas, coal, and oil – for 95 percent of our power, which also generates 30 tons of fumes and soot annually for every Iowan. Some of those emissions trap the sun's heat and add to global climate change. More efficient use of fossil fuels and increased use of renewable energy could reduce those impacts and decrease other pollutants in our air and water.

Energy costs us more than $6 billion each year. We could save 30 percent of what we spend on our utility bills through investments in energy efficiency. Smarter energy use can give us more productivity from every kilowatt-hour we pay for, lessening our impact on the environment while improving our quality of life. We could do more by developing biomass fuels, by continuing farmers' savings through reduced tillage and less fertilizer use, by using existing passive solar techniques, and by further promoting a wind energy industry that's already a leader in the nation. Electric utility deregulation also may provide incentives to use energy carefully and efficiently and to produce power from renewable sources. With good management, our energy future could be brighter.

Coal will be part of our energy mix for some time into the future, but it will not be produced in Iowa. Our state produced more coal than any other state in the late 1800s, but demand faded in the face of alternative fuels and higher quality coal from elsewhere. Our last coal mine closed in 1994. Iowa mining now is focused on limestone, sand, gravel, clay, and gypsum.

While we extract these needed resources from the ground, we also bury others that we consider waste. But, in reality, there's no such thing as "waste" – and no "away" to throw it. Eventually, Iowans must live with or reuse the 4 million tons of garbage we produce annually. Although recycling and waste reduction have cut our landfill use by one-third since 1988, we still dump 2.7 million tons of trash annually, enough to fill 14,400 houses.

Ron Johnson

Recreational opportunities on Iowa's land include numerous bike trails, hiking at Pike's Peak State Park in Clayton County, beach volleyball at Big Creek Lake State Park in Polk County, canoeing along the bedrock palisades of the Upper Iowa River, and fishing the waters of the Middle Raccoon River.

Clay Smith

Ken Formanek

Greg Ludvigson

Ken Formanek

The mandatory deposit on beverage containers has helped. We recycle 92 percent (1.29 billion annually) of the pop and beer cans we use. Since 1979, we have reclaimed one-million cubic yards of aluminum cans, enough to overflow the UNI-Dome. Because it takes 95 percent less energy to make a can from recycled aluminum than from ore, the annual energy savings could power 26,000 homes.

We also have embraced curbside recycling and programs to collect household hazardous wastes. By simply recycling and reusing products and consuming less, Iowans annually save energy equal to 89 million gallons of gasoline.

Businesses and industries also can avoid pollution by developing less hazardous products and processes. With the initial help of outside specialists, companies have saved more than $109 million, while cutting wastes by 1.1 million tons since 1991.

Shopping for low-impact products, recycling, and reduced consumption can save money for individual Iowans and for businesses, while reducing our communities' waste disposal dilemmas.

78

ean C. Prior

Jim Scheffler

Protection of Iowa's historic sites reminds us of the human tenure on the land. Some sites also encourage recreation and tourism, such as the annual rendezvous at Fort Atkinson State Preserve in Winneshiek County (above and near right) and the scenic covered bridges of Madison County. (Hogback Bridge, originally built in 1884, far right)

Clay Smith

Rather than dwell on such environmental problems, we'd sometimes prefer to emphasize what we do best in Iowa, and that is grow things. More than 90 percent of our land produces agricultural crops, trees, or pasture grasses.

But even that land resource is shrinking. Shopping malls, highways, suburbs, and factories now cover three-quarters of a million acres of the state, the equivalent of two counties.

Between 1992 and 1997, we annually lost an area equal to fifty-four average-size farms, more than 18,000 acres.

Iowa's losses may be crucial, because 53 percent of our agricultural land is prime farmland, and development often takes the best land first. Level ground appeals as much to industry and road builders and landscapers and building contractors as it does to farmers.

Conversion of farmland raises other issues. What will it cost to provide services like roads, utilities, and schools to new developments? What are the environmental impacts of developing the land or of the additional miles people drive? Is the

About 9 percent of Iowans live on the farm and interact daily with the land.

That complex land-people relationship will continue to evolve. Iowans are aging, and our population increase is slow. In the next twenty years, we may grow only 3 to 6 percent over the 2.86 million people we had in 1998. We have more residents age seventy-five or older than we do age five or younger. We're becoming more urban, as people move from farms to cities. And our ethnic makeup is becoming more diverse, with increases in the number of Hispanic, African-American, Eastern European, and Asian residents.

These changes could affect our natural resources. More than 90 percent of Iowa's land is privately owned, often by older people. Two-thirds of the land belongs to individuals age

land in a floodplain? Can we ever justify building where water is certain to flow? Aren't open spaces important to our well-being, too?

And how can we protect the wonders of a starry night from the glare of urban illumination? City lights can make the sky fifty times brighter than natural sky, allowing us to see only 200 stars instead of 2,500. We could solve the problem, and save energy, by using lights that are shielded to direct their beams downward.

For the sake of the land and the people who use it, these may be questions worth asking. Once paved or developed, a farm field can almost never be recovered.

80

Marquette, Iowa, in Clayton County characterizes the numerous small towns and communities that dot the Iowa landscape.

*The Iowa Beverage Containers Deposit Law – or
bottle bill as it's commonly known – changed the
way we think about our responsibility to the
environment. It counters a habit of litter and
creates more positive attitudes about taking care
of our beautiful land.
– Robert D. Ray, former Governor of Iowa
Des Moines Register editorial, July 23, 1998*

Drake Hokanson

*The suburbs expanding outward from Iowa's larger metropolitan areas
characterize another way that people live on the land.*

fifty-five and older, while nearly 20 percent belongs to owners over age seventy-four. Thus, one property in five probably will change hands within ten to twenty years, as people die. The new landholders, who may have grown up in urban areas, could decide to use land differently from the older owners, who were more likely to have had long ties to agriculture.

The migration of people from rural areas to cities also may increase pressure to build around urban centers. Polk County, for example, has lost 3,000 acres of open space to development annually since the early 1990s.

As Iowa's population becomes more diverse, people of different cultural and religious backgrounds may look at the land and its resources in different ways. To some Iowans, the land is a resource to be exploited for profit. New residents may bring nontraditional land ethics and customs. To many, land

has spiritual and natural values and should be protected for future generations.

When we choose a home in Iowa – a place still uncluttered and livable – we often do so because we recognize what a treasure we have in this "land between two rivers." Individuals, business people, government leaders, and private interest groups – we all share a vision with people like ourselves. And people will decide how our land is used. We will determine whether our natural communities and human communities will prosper. We will paint a portrait for posterity.

A Vision for Iowa's Land

Monarch butterfly

American kestrel

Butterfly weed

As much as we Iowans like to look back at our proud heritage, to feel the roots that connect us to the land, and to admire what we have built from the abundance that our ancestors found here, we also need to look forward, and to dream.

With *Iowa – Portrait of the Land,* we're asking Iowans to look ahead, just as visionary leaders did when they prepared our first state conservation plan in 1933. In the process, our diverse people will see varied – often overlapping – images of our future, each colored by a different person's background. Families long for safe, happy, healthy lives. Farmers may wish for new crops that require less cultivation and fewer chemicals, promote biological diversity, thrive in all weather, produce large yields, command high prices, and rejuvenate the soil. Teachers seek eager students, supportive parents, understanding commu-

nities, and modern classrooms. Business owners and employees alike depend upon a stable economy.

We're unique, yet alike. Although our visions may diverge, they come into focus on a shared responsibility, a common hope: the quality of our land.

At first, we may look at the land as a history book,

Right: Rooted in an understanding of our land's past, Iowans can look to the future. The land is seen with a sense of connection, protection, and reverence. Iowa can lead by example in the future stewardship of the Earth.

Marlene Ehresman

82

Roger Hill

Right: Iowa's land has seen profound change. As earlier ways of life pass into history, the Earth's cycles and systems still continue around, beneath, and above us. While our children's future will not be our past, we can teach them to value the enduring resources and processes of the land that sustain life.

recording not only the natural events but also the human experiences that have shaped the earth, this state, and our lives. Gradually, however, we're discovering how to understand the more subtle messages, the clues that show and tell us how we can sustain this land for future generations. "Once you learn to read the land, I have no fear of what you will do to it, or with it. And I know many pleasant things it will do to you," said Burlington native Aldo Leopold.

The land is our infrastructure, the physical basis for all we are and for whatever we may become. Urban dwellers depend on the land and its complex parts just as much as rural people do – for the health of our bodies and of our souls. We each need clean water, fresh air, open space, and the chance to touch the natural marvels that surround us. A farmer impulsively climbs down to grab and crumble a handful of soil. A child stares in wonder at a honeybee on a dandelion. Food chains and geology and photosynthesis come alive when young students can plant a tree, frolic in a prairie, or pick up rocks in an unpolluted stream. Workday stresses may melt away on a

stroll through a wooded urban park, a paddle on a quiet river, or a hike along an unmowed country roadside. In a hectic world, we relish simple pleasures, like savoring silence, gazing at the stars, or smelling a spring rain.

And when we touch or smell or see the land, or hear its winds and its animal voices, or taste the food it produces, the soul of that land in turn touches us. We feel a spiritual kinship with the Earth. Perhaps that dream is the one we should strive hardest to attain – the sense of connection to our land. Each of us is a citizen, bonded together in a natural community, with the land at the hub, sharing a dynamic, living landscape.

Our future, like our past, is wedded to that land and to

83

Iowa Dept. of Natural Resources

Roger Hill

Our steps into the future will continue to show us what the word "natural" truly means. Natural places are increasingly unexpected in Iowa, and we risk losing what we don't expect to find.

the people, plants, and animals who live on it, in it, with it, and from it. As just one part of the land, will we be good stewards, good citizens, of that community? Good citizens also respect their neighbors and their property.

Iowans ask much of the land – and the land, in turn, challenges us. We farm the fields, use the water, build the homes and businesses, dig the mineral resources, bury the wastes, and play in the parks. Yet, as we live in and look at

today's Iowa, we must strive to appreciate yesterday and to see tomorrow. Both our past and our future are rooted in Iowa's land and in its ability to work for us and with us. If we understand its geological history and its natural processes, then we can use that knowledge to conserve and renew the land. As we mold and remodel the land to suit our needs, we can help it adapt to the changes we impose upon it. Whether we choose to treat our land gently and with respect, or harshly and callously, we are shaping the legacy we leave for our children.

Will we decide upon clean water, clear air, sustainable farms, vigorous forests and prairies, diverse wildlife, and vibrant cities – or something else? We still have the choice; we can decide, by our action or inaction. Our future, in this vision of connections, is one of opportunity. We have the knowledge not only to repair the damage we already may have done to our land, but also to improve that land and to preserve it for our children. We have the wisdom, if we have the will.

When we know that our land, the quality of our lives, and our livelihoods are intertwined, it will be easier for us to work as partners to improve all three. Farmers can then more fully appreciate the whistle of a meadowlark. Townspeople can share the pride in a family's century farm. We all can live in a state where agriculture is an integral part of a vigorous, lively landscape. Productive farms will blend with stream buffers and roadsides and woodlots and trail corridors. The combination will weave vitality and diversity throughout the agricultural patchwork quilt that blankets much of the state. We will see that "nature" need not be confined to a park or preserve, and that "farming" can mean growing plants and animals whose worth doesn't always have to be measured by dollars and cents. The harvest of Iowa's land can be in commodities set aside for the future. It can be what Aldo Leopold called "an aesthetic harvest" – getting to know and value the land. As we reach for these visions, we'll better ourselves as we maintain the land.

We'll give equal rank to the farm field and to the wetland, although we must measure their production in very different ways. We still may judge a cornfield by bushels harvested, by commodity prices, by fuel and fertilizer inputs, and perhaps by the soil that we retain after the corn is combined. Can we, with equal enthusiasm, judge the marsh in terms of the water it filters, the muskrat population, its reflection of the autumn sunset, or its cacophony of spring bird songs?

What about the prairie relict, still unplowed in the face of progress, or the plot of native grasses and flowers that we have seeded to emulate the prairie? Can we guard the one as jealously as we would a museum of priceless art work, and the other as a living laboratory, an experiment in mimicking the hand of nature?

We will learn to revere the forest, as well as the trees. Some of our woodlands can become parklands, preserves, timber crop producers, songbird sanctuaries, watershed protectors, and nutrient recyclers.

Ancient Indian mounds and village sites will inspire and humble us, as we hear in these historical treasures the voices of

John M. Zielinski

The harvest of Iowa's land can be in commodities set aside for the future. Tomorrow's harvests will depend on individuals who will teach their children to tend the health of the land as a living system.

Lowell Washburn

hundreds of generations of early Iowans. We will reflect on the accomplishments of these early people and learn from their generations of living with the land.

Perhaps we can learn to look at what we now call wastes and consider them resources instead. Livestock manure once again will become a valuable commodity, rather than a pollutant. Industries will profit from their by-products, rather than discarding them. As we move from the throw-away mentality

85

Clay Smith

Large turbines generate power from the wind,
a source of clean, renewable energy.

*Far right: The Hale-Bopp Comet was one of the most
spectacular celestial events of the century. This photograph
was taken Easter Sunday, March 30, 1997, about forty-
five minutes after sunset, and it won "Best of Show for
Photography" at the 1997 Iowa State Fair. The photographer, John Wenck of Des Moines, was looking northwest
over St. Paul's Church about ten miles northeast of Boone.
The historic church, built of wood in 1898, sits on a
prominent knoll of glacial deposits left about 13,500
years earlier.*

*We shall not cease from exploration
And the end of all our exploring
Will be to arrive where we started
And know the place for the first time.
– T. S. Eliot, Little Gidding*

to "reduce, reuse, recycle," we'll have less need for landfills.

In our decidedly rural state, the distinction between
urban and rural may become blurred, as we recognize that our
relationship to the land is only a matter of scale. An urban
resident who grows wildflowers and backyard bird habitat may
develop the same sense of stewardship as a farmer whose
conservation practices make his or her land a model of profitable, sustainable agriculture. We will judge all our land-use
decisions by their effects on the natural community and on our
children's children, rather than solely upon short-term economic gain.

All of us – private citizens, members of conservation and
special interest groups, business leaders, government workers –
will share the responsibility for our past shortcomings and for
the challenge to build a better future.

Once again, Aldo Leopold's words can guide us. His
"land ethic" proposed how we could define conservation, or
harmony with the land. "A thing is right when it tends to
preserve the integrity, stability and beauty of the biotic community," Leopold wrote. "It is wrong when it tends otherwise."

RESOURCES AND REFERENCES

Alex, Lynn M. 2000. *Iowa's Archaeological Past.* University of Iowa Press, Iowa City. 420 p.

America's Private Land, A Geography of Hope. 1997. United States Department of Agriculture, Natural Resources Conservation Service. Washington, D.C. 80 p.

Anderson, Wayne. I. 1998. *Iowa's Geological Past: Three Billion Years of Change.* University of Iowa Press, Iowa City. 424 p.

At Home with Conservation. 1997. Iowa Department of Natural Resources, Des Moines. 23 p.

Bataille, Gretchen M., David M. Gradwohl, and Charles L. P. Silet (editors). 2000. *The Worlds between Two Rivers: Perspectives on American Indians in Iowa.* University of Iowa Press, Iowa City. 232 p.

Bennett, Mary. *An Iowa Album: A Photographic History, 1860-1920.* University of Iowa Press, Iowa City. 344 p., 377 photos.

Black, Gladys. 1992. *Iowa Birdlife.* University of Iowa Press, Iowa City. 176 p.

Bodmer, Karl, Marsha V. Gallagher (photographer), and David C. Hunt (photographer). 1993. *Karl Bodmer's America.* Joslyn Art Museum and University of Nebraska Press, Lincoln. 376 p.

Christiansen, James L. and Reeve M. Bailey. 1988. *The Lizards and Turtles of Iowa.* Nongame Technical Series No. 3. Iowa Department of Natural Resources, Des Moines.

Christiansen, James L. and Reeve M. Bailey. 1990. *The Snakes of Iowa.* Nongame Technical Series No. 1. Iowa Department of Natural Resources, Des Moines.

Christiansen, James L. and Reeve M. Bailey. 1991. *The Salamanders and Frogs of Iowa.* Nongame Technical Series No. 3. Iowa Department of Natural Resources, Des Moines.

Christiansen, Paul, and Mark Müller. 1999. *An Illustrated Guide to Iowa Prairie Plants.* University of Iowa Press, Iowa City. 237 p.

Conard, Rebecca. 1997. *Places of Quiet Beauty: Parks, Preserves, and Environmentalism.* University of Iowa Press, Iowa City. 382 p.

Cooper, Tom C. 1982. *Iowa's Natural Heritage.* Iowa Natural Heritage Foundation and Iowa Academy of Science. 341 p.

Darling Foundation, J. N. "Ding." 785 Crandon Blvd., Suite 1206, Key Biscayne, Florida 33149.

Dinsmore, James J. 1994. *A Country So Full of Game: The Story of Wildlife in Iowa.* University of Iowa Press, Iowa City. 233 p.

Dinsmore, Stephen J., Laura S. Jackson, Bruce L. Ehresman, and James J. Dinsmore. 1995. *Iowa Wildlife Viewing Guide.* Falcon Press Publishing, Inc. Helena and Billings, Montana. 95 p.

Eilers, Lawrence J., and Dean M. Roosa. 1994. *The Vascular Plants of Iowa: An Annotated Checklist and Natural History.* University of Iowa Press, Iowa City. 304 p.

Famous and Historical Trees of Iowa. 1996. Iowa Department of Natural Resources, Des Moines. 38 p. Includes "The Historic Role of Iowa Trees," by Cornelia F. Mutel, p. 4-16.

Garvin, Paul. 1998. *Iowa's Minerals: Their Occurrence, Origins, Industries, and Lore.* University of Iowa Press, Iowa City. 260 p.

Harlan, J. R., E. V. Speaker, and J. Mayhew. 1987. *Iowa Fish and Fishing.* Iowa Department of Natural Resources, Des Moines. 323 p.

Hokanson, Drake. 1994. *Reflecting a Prairie Town, A Year in Peterson.* University of Iowa Press, Iowa City. 259 p.

Huffman, Donald M., George Knaphus, and Lois H. Tiffany. 1989. *Mushrooms and Other Fungi of the Midcontinental United States.* Iowa State University Press, Ames. 362 p.

Iowa Comparative Risk Project, Final Report [Assessment of Environmental Issues]. 1999. Iowa Department of Natural Resources, Des Moines. 58 p.

Iowa Conservationist. Iowa Department of Natural Resources, Des Moines. (Bimonthly)

Iowa Energy Plan Update and Data Addendum. 2000. Iowa Department of Natural Resources, Des Moines. 40 p.

Iowa Geology. Iowa Department of Natural Resources, Geological Survey Bureau. Iowa City. (Annual)

Iowa Renewable Energy Resource Guide. 1999. Iowa Department of Natural Resources, Des Moines. 55 p.

Jackson, Laura Spess, Carol A. Thompson, and James J. Dinsmore. 1996. *The Iowa Breeding Bird Atlas.* University of Iowa Press, Iowa City. 484 p.

Kent, Thomas H., and James J. Dinsmore. 1996. *Birds in Iowa.* Published by the authors, Iowa City and Ames. 391 p.

Kurtz, Carl. 1996. *Iowa's Wild Places.* Iowa State University Press and Iowa Natural Heritage Foundation. 236 p.

Lannoo, Michael J. 1996. *Okoboji Wetlands, A Lesson in Natural History.* University of Iowa Press, Iowa City. 156 p.

Laubach, Christyna M., John B. Bowles, and René Laubach. 1994. *A Guide to the Bats of Iowa.* Nongame Technical Series No. 2. Iowa Department of Natural Resources, Des Moines.

Leopold, Aldo. 1933. The conservation ethic. *Journal of Forestry* 31:634-647.

Leopold, Aldo. 1966. *A Sand County Almanac, With Essays on Conservation from Round River.* Oxford University Press, Inc., New York. 295 p.

Madson, John. 1982. *Where the Sky Began: Land of the Tallgrass Prairie.* Houghton Mifflin, Boston. 321 p.

Müller, Mark, 2000. *Prairie in Your Pocket, A Guide to Plants of the Tallgrass Prairie.* University of Iowa Press. Iowa City.

Mutel, Cornelia F. 1989. *Fragile Giants, A Natural History of the Loess Hills.* University of Iowa Press, Iowa City. 284 p.

Mutel, Cornelia F., and Mary Swander (editors). 1994. *Land of the Fragile Giants: Landscapes, Environments, and Peoples of the Loess Hills.* Published for the Brunnier Art Museum at Iowa State University by the University of Iowa Press, Iowa City. 117 p.

Oschwald, W. R., F. F. Riecken, R. I. Dideriksen, W. H. Scholtes, and F. W. Schaller. 1965. *Principal Soils of Iowa.* Iowa State University Cooperative Extension Service, Special Report No. 42, Ames. 76 p.

Outdoor Adventure Guide. 1997. Iowa Association of Conservation Boards, 405 SW 3rd St., Suite 1, Ankeny 50021 or your local conservation board, 168 p.

Pammel, L. H., J. F. Ford, J. Kelso, and E. R. Harlan. 1919. *Public Parks of Iowa.* The State of Iowa, Des Moines. 328 p.

Plowden, David. 1988. *A Sense of Place.* State Historical Society of Iowa in association with W.W. Norton and Company, New York. 158 p.

Prior, Jean C. 1991. *Landforms of Iowa.* University of Iowa Press, Iowa City. 153 p.

Reece, Maynard. *Dark Sky – Canvasbacks.* © Maynard Reece by arrangement with Mill Pond Press Inc., 204 S. Nassau Street, Venice, Florida 33595.

Report on the Iowa Twenty-Five Year Conservation Plan. 1933. Iowa Board of Conservation and Iowa Fish and Game Commission. 176 p.

Runkel, Sylvan T., and Alvin F. Bull. 1979. *Wildflowers of Iowa Woodlands.* Iowa State University Press, Ames. 264 p.

Runkel, Sylvan T., and Dean M. Roosa, 1989. *Wildflowers of the Tallgrass Prairie.* Iowa State University Press, Ames. 279 p.

Runkel, Sylvan T., and Dean M. Roosa. 1999. *Wildflowers and Other Plants of Iowa Wetlands.* Iowa State University Press, Ames. 372 p.

Sage, Leland L. 1974. *A History of Iowa.* Iowa State University Press, Ames. 376 p.

Schwieder, Dorothy. 1996. *Iowa: The Middle Land.* Iowa State University Press, Ames. 381 p.

Shirley, Shirley. 1994. *Restoring the Tallgrass Prairie: An Illustrated Manual for Iowa and the Upper Midwest.* University of Iowa Press, Iowa City. 330 p.

Stone, Larry A. 1999. *Listen to the Land.* Mid-Prairie Books, Parkersburg, Iowa. 225 p.

Thompson, Janette R. 1992. *Prairies, Forests, and Wetlands: The Restoration of Natural Landscape Communities in Iowa.* University of Iowa Press, Iowa City. 139 p.

United States Department of Agriculture, Natural Resources Conservation Service. 1999. *Summary Report, 1997 National Resources Inventory.* 84 p.

Van der Linden, Peter J., and Donald R. Farrar. 1993. *Forest and Shade Trees of Iowa.* Iowa State University Press, Ames. 133 p.

Winkler, Suzanne. 1997. *The Smithsonian Guides to Natural America: the Heartland.* Smithsonian Books, Washington D.C., Random House, New York, p. 82-120.

ACKNOWLEDGEMENTS

Paul W. Johnson – *Director, Iowa Department of Natural Resources (IDNR)*

Jean Cutler Prior – *Project Coordinator, Editor; Geological Survey IDNR*
Jerry A. Kemperman – *Project Coordinator, Forests and Prairies IDNR*
Larry A. Stone – *Lead Writer, Elkader, Iowa*
Patricia J. Lohmann – *Publication Designer, IDNR*
Mark Müller – *Iowa flora and fauna illustrations, Cosgrove, Iowa*
Teresa Hay McMahon – *Special Assistant, IDNR*

PROJECT COMMITTEE

Brian Button – *Environmental Protection IDNR*
Dale J. Ceolla – *Natural Resources Conservation Service, USDA*
Tammra K. Foster – *Energy IDNR*
Dale Garner – *Wildlife IDNR*
Kathy Gourley – *State Historical Society, Iowa Department of Cultural Affairs*
William Green – *State Archaeologist, University of Iowa*
Ruth Herzberg – *Parks, Recreation, and Preserves IDNR*
Leslie Leager – *Waste Management IDNR*
Larry Mitzner – *Fisheries IDNR*
John Walkowiak – *Forestry Services IDNR*

Cover
Design by Patricia J. Lohmann
Prairie photographs by Roger Hill
Prairie grass illustrations by Mark Müller

Title page
Photograph of prairie plants by Ty Smedes

SUPPORT PROVIDED BY

Iowa Chapter of The Nature Conservancy
Iowa Natural Heritage Foundation
Iowa Recycling Association
Izaak Walton League of America, Iowa Division
Pheasants Forever

If you have ideas, comments, questions, or suggestions
concerning the future of Iowa's land and its natural resources,
write and let us know.

To send comments or to order this publication:

Iowa Department of Natural Resources
Wallace State Office Building
502 East 9th St.
Des Moines, IA 50319-0034

515-281-5918 (orders only)

www.state.ia.us/dnr